The Interior Castle

Modern update of the spiritual guide
by Teresa of Ávila

M.B. Anderson

Copyright ©2022 Root Classics

All rights reserved. No part of this publication may be reproduced, distributed, or transmitted in any form or by any means, including photocopying, recording, or other electronic or mechanical methods, without the prior written permission of the publisher, except in the case of brief quotations embodied in critical reviews and certain other noncommercial uses permitted by copyright law.

For permission requests, contact the publisher at the domain address below.

ISBN: 978-1-956314-01-4 (paperback)

Library of Congress Control Number: 2022901894

Edited by Rhode St. Genese

Cover design by Wayne Slezak

First edition

Root Classics
Barrington, IL
www.RootClassics.com

Contents

Prologue	1
The First Mansion	5
One	6
Two	12
The Second Mansion	23
The Third Mansion	33
One	34
Two	41
The Fourth Mansion	51
One	52
Two	60
Three	66
The Fifth Mansion	77
One	78
Two	86
Three	94
Four	101
The Sixth Mansion	107
One	108
Two	117
Three	122
Four	131
Five	140
Six	146
Seven	154
Eight	163
Nine	170
Ten	180
Eleven	184
The Seventh Mansion	191
One	192
Two	199
Three	206
Four	214
Epilogue	223

Note

In 1577, Teresa of Ávila, a Spanish Carmelite nun, was asked by her superiors to write a spiritual guide for her Carmelite sisters. Her teaching, *The Interior Castle*, is now among the most widely read and studied Christian mystical texts. This paraphrased version stays true to the text, but simple structure and contemporary word choices make it easier for modern readers to understand.

Identifying the soul as a castle, Teresa outlines seven "Mansions" within the castle, illustrating the beauty and capacity of the soul. The descriptions of the first three Mansions are brief and explain how the soul benefits from spiritual effort and the help of God's grace. But Teresa's focus is on helping us understand the remaining Mansions, where the inward journey deepens.

A prolific writer, Teresa also was a reformer who founded numerous convents throughout Spain. She must have understood the risk of producing a book exploring mystical topics in the shadow of both the Reformation and the Spanish Inquisition. Four centuries later, Teresa was recognized as one of the few women "doctors" of the Catholic Church – a title given to Catholic saints who made great contributions to theology or doctrine.

Prologue

Rarely has obedience laid such a difficult task on me as this writing about prayer. First, I do not feel God has given me either the power or desire for this work. And second, in the past three months I have suffered from noises and a great weakness in my head that have made it painful to write even on necessary business.

However, I know that the power of obedience can make things that seem impossible easy. So, I resolve to carry out the task willingly, even though I am distressed by my struggle with sickness and other duties. For the Lord has not given me enough virtue to overcome the reluctance of my nature. May He, in whose mercy I trust and who in kindness has helped me in many other difficult duties, do this work for me.

I think I have little to add to what I have already written. In fact, I am afraid I will just repeat myself. I am like a parrot who knows how to talk but who only knows what it has heard, so it says the same thing over and over.

If the Lord wishes me to write anything new, He will teach it to me or bring back a memory of something I said in the past, for I would even be content with this. I am very forgetful, so I will be glad to repeat things that I was told were well said. If our Lord does not grant me this, but I weary my brains and increase my headache striving to obey, I will gain in merit, even if my words are useless to anyone.

And so, I am beginning to comply today, on the feast of the Blessed Trinity, in the year 1577, in this Carmelite monastery of Saint Joseph in Toledo, where I am presently. I submit all my writings to the judgment of those who order me to write, because they are men of great learning.

It will be the fault of ignorance, not malice, if I say anything contrary to the doctrine of the holy Roman Catholic Church. By God's goodness I am and always will be faithful to the Church. May He be forever blessed and glorified, amen.

He who asks me to write this tells me that some of the sisters in the convents of our Lady of Carmel need help overcoming their difficulties with prayer. He believes women will better understand each other's language, and that since they have special affection for me, they will pay more attention to my words. I thus understand it is important for me to write this, and I will be speaking to my sisters as I write. The idea that anyone else could benefit by what I say would be absurd.

Our Lord will do me a great favor if He enables me to help even one of my sisters praise Him a little more. His Majesty knows I have no other goal. It should be very clear that if I manage to say anything helpful, it did not come from me. With my small understanding and skill, I can write nothing of the sort, unless the Lord gives it to me.

The First Mansion

One

I begged our Lord today to speak through me. I do not know what to say or how to begin this work that has been laid upon me by obedience. While I prayed, a thought occurred to me that I will now set down and which will be the foundation on which to build.

I saw the soul as if it resembled a Castle made from a single diamond or of very clear crystal. And within this single sparkling diamond are many Mansions, each with many rooms, just as in heaven there are many Mansions.

Our Interior Castle

Now think about this carefully, sisters. Our redeemed soul is a paradise – a diamond Castle – in which God says He finds delight.[1] And what do you think a castle would be like which is the delight of a King so mighty, so wise, so pure, and so full of all that is good? Nothing can compare with the great beauty and spaciousness of that Castle, our soul.

Even if we had superior intelligence, we are as unable to understand the great beauty of our soul as we are unable to understand God. And this makes sense – He told us He created us in His own image and likeness.[2]

Now if this is so – and it is – there is no reason to tire ourselves trying to grasp the beauty of this Castle, our soul. Since this Castle is a creature, there is as much of a difference

---

[1] Proverbs 8:31
[2] Genesis 1:26

between it and God, as between His creation and the Creator. The very fact that His Majesty says the soul is made in His image means we can hardly comprehend our soul's great dignity and beauty.

It is such a pity and disgrace that through our own fault we do not understand ourselves. Wouldn't it show ignorance, my daughters, if a person were asked who he was, and he said he had no idea – that he did not know who his parents were or what country he came from?

Our own ignorance is much greater. We make no attempt to discover who we really are. We assume we only have these bodies and some vague idea of a "soul" inside of us because someone told us we should believe this.

But we rarely even think about our souls – the gifts they possess, who dwells in them and how precious they are. So we don't take the trouble to preserve and deepen our soul's beauty. Our energy is focused on the rough setting of the diamond, the outer wall of the Castle – these bodies of ours.

Favors in the Castle's Mansions

Let us now imagine that this Castle, as I have said, contains many Mansions – some above, below, and at each side. But in the center and midst of them all is the main Mansion where the most secret things pass between God and our soul.

Think about this comparison carefully. Maybe through what I explain, God will be pleased to show you the different favors He wishes to give our souls. No one can ever fully understand all these favors, especially someone as ignorant as I.

The knowledge that such favors from God are possible will be a great consolation to you. And if you do not receive them all, you can still praise Him for His great goodness in giving them to others. Thinking about the blessings of heaven does not harm us. It should cheer us toward the joy ahead. And thinking about the blessings we have now to commune with God, despite our unworthiness, should cause us to love Him for his great goodness and infinite mercy.

If anyone is upset that God gives these favors to the souls of others in this exile on earth but not to themselves, then they lack humility and love of their neighbors. We should be glad that others receive these favors. In no way does it reduce God's capacity to give us this favor as well. We should rejoice that His greatness is on display wherever He chooses.[3]

Sometimes He gives these favors to our soul only to demonstrate His power. When Jesus healed the blind man, His disciples asked if the man lost his sight because of his sins or those of his parents.[4] Jesus replied that the man was blind only so he could be healed, and God's greatness be known.

And God does not grant these favors only to those who are "holier." He grants them in order for His greatness to be made known (consider Saint Paul and Mary Magdalen), so that we would praise Him for His work in His creatures.

Some may say that these favors to the soul cannot come from God and are beyond the clear teaching of our faith. But it is better that those weak in faith should doubt us than that

[3] Matthew 20:15
[4] John 9:2

we stop teaching about spiritual favors to benefit those who receive them. Those who receive these favors rejoice and try to love God better and awaken others to a fresh love of Him who grants such mercies through His power and majesty.

But I know none of you to whom I speak doubts the truth of what I will share about our interior Castle. You know and believe even greater proofs of His love. And if you doubt, then learn from experience. Since God has no limits to His work, do not discredit what you have not experienced.

Entering our Interior Castle

Now let us return to our beautiful and delightful Castle and discover how to enter. This may sound like nonsense, for if this Castle is our soul, then of course we can enter. For we ourselves are the Castle, and it would be absurd to tell someone to enter a room he is already in!

But you must understand that there are many ways of "being" in this Castle. Many souls remain in the outer court of the Castle, which is the place occupied by the guards. The guards are not interested in entering the soul. They have no idea what is in the wonderful Castle, who dwells there or even how many rooms it has. But the soul must enter itself, just as certain books on prayer advise.

A short time ago I was told by a great teacher that souls without prayer are like people whose bodies or limbs are paralyzed. They have hands and feet, but they cannot control them. In the same way, there are souls so weak and busy with the cares of the world that nothing can be done for them. Distractions make them incapable of entering within themselves. They are so accustomed to living with the reptiles and other creatures found in the outer court of the Castle that they have begun to imitate them.

And although these souls hold the rich power of conversing with none other than God Himself, they are hopeless to lay hold of this. Unless they work hard to realize and remedy their miserable condition, they will be turned into pillars of salt for not looking within themselves, just as Lot's wife was turned into salt because she looked back at Sodom.[5]

As far as I can understand, the gate of entry into this Castle is prayer and meditation. I am not saying it is more mental than vocal prayer, but prayer in which the mind must take part. Moving your lips is not prayer. A person prays when they think about Whom they are addressing, what they are asking for, and who they are that venture to speak with God.

True, it is sometimes possible to pray without paying attention to these things, but this only comes with practice. A person is not praying at all if they are in the habit of speaking to God as freely as they would speak to their servant, never wondering whether the words are suitable, or only saying words they have learned by heart. No Christian should ever speak to God in this way! At any rate, sisters, I hope to God that none of you will, for we often talk about spiritual matters, which is a good way to protect ourselves from these bad habits.

Let us say no more about these paralyzed souls, who,

---

[5] Genesis 19:26

unless the Lord Himself comes and commands them to rise, are like the man who lay beside the pool for over thirty years.[6] They are quite unfortunate and live in great danger.

Let us think about other souls, who do at last enter the Castle. Their intentions are good, but they are still absorbed in the cares of the world. Sometimes, although not often since they are very busy, they talk to our Lord, and think about the state of their souls, although not very carefully. When they do pray a few times a month, their minds are full of a thousand preoccupations. Their thoughts reflect their attachments, for, where their treasure is, there their heart is also.[7]

From time to time, however, they are able to shake their minds free. It is a great thing when they know themselves well enough to know they are lost and unable to reach the Castle gate. Eventually they enter the first rooms in the basement of the Castle, but so many reptiles get in with them that they can't appreciate the beauty of the Castle or find any peace within its walls. Still, it is an accomplishment to enter.

You may think, daughters, that this does not concern you because by God's grace you are further inside the Castle. But you must be patient, for there is no other way to understand our interior Castle without understanding this first Mansion. May it please the Lord to help me to explain these things to you. Some of these ideas are difficult to understand without personal experience. And sometimes we also touch on subjects which, by His mercy, will never concern us.

[6] John 5:5-9
[7] Matthew 6:21

Two

Souls Separated from God

Before moving on, let us talk about the state of this beautiful Castle, this pearl from the Orient, this tree of life, planted in the living water of life – namely, in God – when it commits willful sin.[8] No thicker darkness exists. Even though the Sun himself is still at the center of the soul, the soul is unable to share in the light. The soul's crystal is unable to reflect the light from the center of the soul.

While in this state of willful disobedience, the soul cannot find satisfaction in anything. Even if that soul does good works, the works do not flow from God, who alone is the source of good. And this soul is separated from Him because it is choosing sin over pleasing Him. It chooses darkness and becomes darkness.

I know of a person to whom our Lord wanted to reveal what a soul was like separated by willful sin. She said that if others understood this, they would find it impossible to purposefully sin again, and they would be prepared to undergo great trials to avoid sin. The Lord gave her a great desire that all might understand this truth. May He give you, daughters, the desire to pray earnestly to God for those who are blind in their darkness.

When it is covered by God's grace, the soul is like the waters that flow in a crystal-clear spring, pleasing to God and

---

[8] Psalm 1:3

man. The soul is rooted like a tree beside the River of Life. The nourishment from these waters causes the tree to provide shade and yield fruit.

On the other hand, when the soul by its own choice leaves this spring and becomes rooted in a black and foul-smelling pool, it produces nothing but misery and filth.

It should be noted here that the brilliant sun at the center of the soul never loses its splendor and beauty. Nothing can take away its loveliness, and it is always present in the soul. But if a thick black cloth is placed over a crystal in the sunshine, no matter how brightly the sun shines, it can't be reflected in the crystal.

Oh, souls redeemed by the blood of Jesus Christ! Learn to understand and take pity on yourselves! Surely, wouldn't you do everything possible to remove the pitch that blackens the crystal? Remember, if your life were to end now, you would never enjoy this light again.

Oh, Jesus! How sad it is to see a soul separated from Your light! What a state the poor rooms of the Castle are in! How distracted are the senses that inhabit the Castle! And the powers of the soul, which are their governors and butlers and stewards – how blind and poorly managed they are! What kind of fruit can be borne by a tree rooted in evil?

I once heard a spiritual man say that he was astonished that a soul in darkness did not slide into actions of greater evil. May God, in His mercy, deliver us from this possibility. For there is nothing in life worth the eternal consequences of willful sin. It is because of this darkness, daughters, that we should walk in fear, and beg God to deliver us. For we are weakness itself, and unless He defends our Castle, we will labor in vain to defend it.[9]

The person who was given a vision of sin said this favor taught her two truths. First, she understood how much sin offended God. She learned to have great reverence and intense fear of offending Him.

Second, the understanding of her sin became a mirror of humility. It made her realize that any good things we do are not possibly from our self, but from the waters of grace and the Sun which gives radiance to our works. This became so clear to her that whenever she did any good action, she immediately thanked the Source, realizing how powerless she was without His help. And she only praised God, never giving a thought to her part in the good deed.

If we can remember these two truths, sisters, then the time you have spent reading this and the time I have spent writing this will not have been lost. Wise and educated men know these truths quite well, but we who are less educated are slow and need instruction in everything. Perhaps this is why our Lord suggested these comparisons to me. May He give us grace to learn from them.

These interior matters are so obscure to the mind that anyone with as little learning as I will have to say many things to get the point across. Whoever reads this must have patience with me, as I have had with myself when writing about things of which I know nothing.

I sometimes take up my paper, like a perfect fool, with no

---

[9] Psalm 127:1

idea of what to say or of how to begin. I fully realize how important it is for you that I should explain the Lord's work in our souls to the best of my ability. For although we continually hear what a good thing prayer is, and our occupation obliges us to engage in it for many hours each day, we know so very little about the supernatural work done by the Lord in the soul and what part we take in it.

Learning about this heavenly interior building will give us great comfort. Despite the fact that our soul is in us, we have very little understanding. Our Lord helped me understand some of these principles which I shared in previous writings, but I have a better understanding now, even of some of the most difficult ideas. Yet I am too ignorant to add to many subjects that are well known.

The Capacity of the Soul

Let us now turn back to our Castle with its many Mansions. Do not imagine these Mansions as arranged in a row, one behind another. Fix your attention on the center, the palace occupied by the King. Think of a fruit, with outer rinds surrounding a savory center. The outer rind must be taken away before the center can be eaten. In the same way, all around this central palace are many Mansions.

In speaking of the soul, always think of it as spacious, ample, and large. The soul's capacity is much greater than we can imagine, and this Sun, which is in the central palace, can reach every part of it.

It is very important for any soul who practices prayer, whether a lot or a little, not to hold itself back and stay in one room. Since God has given our souls such freedom, it must be allowed to roam through the rooms in these Mansions – those above, below and on either side. Do not force it to stay a long time in any one room. It is, however, important to spend a lot of time in the room of self-knowledge.

Self-knowledge

How necessary is the room of self-knowledge! Self-knowledge – the humble knowledge of our complete dependency on God – is essential even if you have been brought into the center of the Castle where He resides. Nothing else perfects the soul as much as the humility that comes from self-knowledge. And let humility always be at work, like a bee in the honeycomb.

But remember, the bee sometimes leaves its hive to look for flowers. Likewise, the soul in the room of self-knowledge should sometimes stop thinking about itself and rise in meditation on the majesty of God. Doing this will help the soul realize its low position better than just through self-examination.

Meditating on God's majesty also frees us from the reptiles that enter the room where self-knowledge is first acquired. And while through God's mercy the soul studies itself, too much self-examination can be as bad as too little. Believe me, we will reach greater heights of virtue by also thinking about God instead of just fixing our eyes on ourselves and our little plot of ground.

I do not know if I have explained this clearly. Self-knowledge – the knowledge of our humble position in relation to our Creator – is critical. Even if you are lifted to heaven in prayer, so long as we are on this earth, nothing is more necessary than humility.

So, I repeat that it is a very good thing – excellent, indeed – to begin by entering the room where humility is practiced, rather than rushing off to the other rooms. This is the way to make progress to deeper Mansions. If we have a safe, level road to walk along, why should we desire wings to fly? Let us strive to make progress in self-knowledge.

There are two advantages to this practice of self-knowledge. First, anything white looks whiter against something black, just as anything black looks blacker against the white. As I see it, we will never succeed in knowing ourselves unless we seek to know God. Let us think about His greatness and see the contrast of our lowliness; look at His purity to see our filth; meditate upon His humility, to see how far we are from being humble.

The second advantage to the practice of self-knowledge is that as we turn from self toward God, we become more courageous and prepared for every good. We suffocate ourselves when we never raise our minds above our own miseries.

We have said how the streams that flow from souls in willful sin are black and foul-smelling. Similarly, although God forbid this is not the same thing – so long as we are buried in thinking about our weakness, these streams of ours will never flow free from the mud of our timid, weak, and fearful thoughts.

We will always be glancing around and saying: Are people

noticing me or not? If I take this path, will harm come to me? Is pride leading me to begin such and such a task? With all my faults, how can I teach others about spiritual things? If I don't follow the crowd, will people think I am trying to act like I am better? Should I avoid extremes, even in the practice of virtue, so I will not risk failure and harm good people? How can someone like me think they could be special?

Oh, God help us, my daughters, what great loss the devil causes with these thoughts! We are led to believe that these misgivings arise from humility, but they come from our lack of self-knowledge. They come from self-absorption and a distorted idea of our own nature. If we think like this, we can never get free of ourselves. This lack of freedom is what should be feared.

It is for this reason, daughters, that I say we must set our eyes upon Christ our good, from whom we shall learn true humility, and upon the example set by His saints. When we have true humility, our minds become courageous. True self-knowledge does not make us fearful.

Although this is only the first Mansion, it contains great riches and treasures. But you must avoid all the reptiles dwelling there and get past them to progress to other Mansions. Terrible are the crafts and wiles that the devil uses to prevent souls from learning to know themselves and understand his tricks.

What a miserable life we lead! In other writings I have spoken on the harm that comes to us when we do not properly understand humility and self-knowledge, so I will say no more here. My daughters, may the Lord grant that something I have said is helpful to you.

Struggles in the First Mansion

I can give you very useful information from my own experience of the first Mansion. I must tell you, for example, that each Mansion contains not just a few rooms, but a very large number of rooms.

There are many ways in which souls enter the rooms of the first Mansion, always with good intentions. But the devil is angry when we enter and has legions of evil spirits hidden in these rooms to stop the progress of Christians from one room to another. And we, poor souls, fail to realize this and are tricked by all kinds of deceptions.

The devil is less successful with those who are in Mansions nearer the King's dwelling-place. But in this first Mansion the soul is still absorbed with ambition for honor and pleasure. Such a soul is easily entrapped even while it may desire to please God and perform good works.

Those who find themselves in this state have little strength to defend themselves. They must often ask for help from His Majesty and take His blessed Mother and His saints as intercessors to fight for them. Truly this is necessary in every state of life, for our help comes only from God. May His Majesty through His mercy grant us this. Amen!

Notice that the light that comes from the center room occupied by the King hardly reaches this first Mansion at all. Although rooms in the first Mansion are not dark and black, as when the soul is in a state of sin, they are to some extent darkened, so that the soul can scarcely see anything.

This is not because there is something wrong with the rooms in the first Mansion. Rather, so many bad things – snakes, vipers, and poisonous creatures – have entered the rooms, preventing the soul from seeing the light. Though the room itself is flooded with sunlight, their eyes are so full of dust they can hardly be opened.

The rooms in the first Mansion are light enough, but beginners cannot enjoy the light because they must pay attention to the wild beasts and animals they have allowed to enter. Though the soul is not in a bad state, it is so preoccupied with possessions, honor, and business affairs that, although it sincerely would like to gaze at the Castle and enjoy its beauty, it is prevented by these distractions and quite unable to free itself.

Everyone who wishes to enter the second Mansion will be well advised, as far as their state of life permits, to try to remove unnecessary consuming cares. I believe this is essential for those who hope to remain in the first Mansion or go deeper in the soul's Castle. For even though the soul has entered the Castle, it is not free from the danger of losing what it has already gained. For in the first Mansion, it can't escape being bitten by the poisonous things surrounding them.

What would happen, then, daughters, if we who are free from these obstacles and have already traveled further into other secret Mansions of the Castle, should deliberately return to the distractions found in the first Mansion? Because of our sin, there are many persons who received spiritual favors who fell back into this misery through their own fault.

In this convent we have freedom from many outward concerns. May it please the Lord to also make us free in regard to inward things, and to deliver us from evil. Beware, my daughters, of cares that have nothing to do with you.

Remember that the struggle with demons continues through nearly all the Mansions in the Castle. Fortunately, in some of them, the Castle guards – who are the powers of our soul – have the strength to fight.

But we can never become careless in recognizing the tricks of the devil since he disguises himself as an angel of light.[10] There are a multitude of ways he harms us, and he creeps into our Castle gradually. We often do not discover him until it is too late. As I told you before, he secretly and silently works his way in, and we must always be on the lookout.

To explain this, I will give you examples of how the devil can undermine the harmony and purpose of our sisters. The devil's aim is to cool the charity and love among us.

In one sister, he reminds her of her sin so that she has no peace unless she is punishing herself. This begins to affect her health, and she is unable to fulfill her duties to support her sisters. You see how something that seems good can end up.

The devil tells another sister that religious perfection is important – which is true – but she begins to judge her sisters. She looks for every fault, criticizes, and runs to inform the prioress. But she may fail to see her own faults. Her sisters only see bad intentions and do not take her actions kindly.

---

[10] 2 Corinthians 11:14

The devil might also use this temptation when reporting our sister's faults to the prioress. This should always be handled with discretion, but if a sister violates a rule of our order then it should not be overlooked, and she should be spoken to. If she does not amend her ways, then for her own good, superiors need to be informed. For the good of the sister, you should speak up about what you see.

However, to prevent deception by the devil, sisters must not gossip and spread rumors. When they do, the devil gains an advantage and nurtures habits of slander. Private matters should be discussed only with the person concerned. Thankfully, in our order we have vows to keep almost continuous silence, but while we have less temptation to gossip, we should still be on our guard.

Let us realize, my daughters, that true perfection consists in love of God and our neighbor. The more perfectly we observe these two commandments, the nearer to perfection we will be. The rules of our religious order are only ways to follow these two commands.

Let us refrain from devotion which leads to indiscreet criticism and let each one of you look first at your own faults. As I have said a great deal to you about this elsewhere, I will not enlarge on it further. I never want you to forget the importance of our mutual love. For if the soul goes about looking for minor faults in others (which sometimes may not be faults at all), it may lose its own peace of mind and perhaps disturb the peace of others. See, then, how costly this kind of perfection can be!

The Second Mansion

Let us now consider souls who enter the second Mansion and what a soul does in those rooms. I will not say a lot about this Mansion because I have written about it elsewhere, and my bad memory will cause me to repeat myself. If I could explain this in a fresh way, you will likely not mind hearing about it again, just as we never tire of books that teach about this, numerous though they are.

The Lord's Call

The second Mansion is occupied by those who have begun to practice prayer. They realize the importance of moving on from the rooms in the first Mansion, but because they do not avoid sin, they lack the determination to not return. This is a very perilous condition. It is a great mercy when they sometimes understand their danger and escape from the snakes and other poisonous creatures surrounding them. But unfortunately, this understanding does not last.

In some ways, souls in the second Mansion are in less danger, but they suffer more than those in the first Mansion. They now understand their danger and hope they can travel further into the Castle. But they suffer more because their hearing was dampened in the first Mansion by the distractions around them. The soul in the first Mansion is like someone who is deaf and unable to speak. But in the second Mansion they can hear, making the trial much harder to bear.

Even so, this is no reason to envy those who are deaf, for it is a wonderful thing to hear what is being said. The souls in the second Mansion now hear the voice of the Lord when He calls. As they get nearer to the place where His Majesty dwells, He becomes a loving Neighbor, and in the second Mansion they learn to recognize His voice.

But in this Mansion, souls are still consumed by the amusements, business affairs, pleasures, and vanities of this world. The creatures surrounding them are so venomous and active that it is almost impossible not to fall in and out of sin.

Despite all this, our Lord is anxious that we should seek Him and enjoy His company. He never stops calling us to come nearer. His voice is so sweet that the poor soul is consumed with grief at its reluctance to respond to Him immediately. It suffers more than if it could not hear Him at all.

The divine communications and calls received in this second Mansion are not the same as those I will describe later. In this Mansion, God speaks to souls through the words of good people, from sermons or books, from other things that are heard, or through illness and trials. Or He may teach a truth during brief moments spent in prayer, for however feeble such prayers may be, God holds them very dear.

Sisters, do not underestimate these first spiritual favors, and do not be discouraged if you don't respond immediately to the Lord's calls. For His Majesty is willing to wait for us many days and even many years, especially when He sees perseverance and good desires in our heart. And perseverance is important at this stage. There is always gain from our resolve.

Nevertheless, in the second Mansion the devil's attacks on the soul are terrible, and the soul suffers more than in the first Mansion. For in the first Mansion the soul was mute and deaf

– or at least it could hear very little. Thus, it offered little resistance to sin, like one who has lost the hope of victory. But in the second Mansion, the understanding is sharper, and the reason and intellect are more alert. The clash of arms and the noise of cannons are so loud that the soul can't help hearing them.

And here the devils turn reptiles loose – that is, deceptive thoughts about the world and eternal joy. The devils remind us how good it is when people praise us for our achievements. They tell us about the risk of giving up our earthly treasures, which the soul wants to do when it first enters this Mansion. The devils place a thousand barriers in our path.

Oh, Jesus! What confusion is created in the poor souls in this Mansion. How distressed they are, not knowing if they should proceed or return to the first Mansion.

Progress and Perseverance

But reason tells the soul that it is a mistake to believe that earthly things are of the slightest value compared to what it is seeking. Faith instructs the soul on where to find true satisfaction.

Memory reminds the soul how all earthly joy ends. We recall someone who lived comfortably who suddenly died and was quickly forgotten. And we recall other prosperous people who are now beneath the ground, and we trample upon their graves where their bodies have returned to the earth.

Our will inclines the soul to love our Lord. We long to return to Him who has given us so many proofs of His love.

In particular, the will shows the soul how this true Lover never leaves but goes with it everywhere and gives it life and being.

Then our intellect comes forward and helps the soul to realize that, for however many years it may live, it can never hope to have a better friend than our Lord. We realize that the world is full of falsehood. The worldly pleasures pictured by the devil are accompanied by troubles, cares, and annoyances in disguise.

Reason convinces the soul that outside this Castle it will find neither security nor peace. It should stop going into strange houses when its own house is full of blessings to be enjoyed now. How fortunate it is when we realize that all we need is in our Castle. And there is a Host of the Castle who will give us all we desire, unless, like the prodigal son, we decide to live elsewhere and feed with the swine.[11]

In the second Mansion, it is reflections of this kind that vanquish devils. But, oh, my Lord and my God, how the world's habit of pursuing vanity ruins everything! So dead is our faith that we trust more in visible vanities, even after we see those who pursue them only discover misfortune. All this is the result of deceptive thoughts. For unless we are careful, these poisonous thoughts will hurt our soul in the same way that a man bitten by a viper finds his entire body poisoned and swollen.

Obviously, a great deal of care is necessary to cure this condition, and only the great mercy of God will preserve us

---

[11] Luke 15:16

from death. Indeed, the soul suffers great trials in this Mansion, especially if the devil sees progress in character and habits. All the powers of hell will join to drive it back again.

Oh, my Lord! It is here that we need Your help. Without it, we have no power. In Your mercy, do not allow this soul to be deceived when its journey has just begun. Give it light to see all that is good within this Castle, and that its welfare requires perseverance and good company.

It is a wonderful thing for beginners to learn from those who know this interior Castle. And not just from those who can be found in the same room, but those who have traveled further into the Castle, for they will be of great help and encouragement.

The soul should resolve itself to lose life and comfort rather then return to the first Mansion. If the devil sees this resolve, he will soon stop troubling him. Let the soul be courageous, not like the soldier who knelt to drink from the brook.[12] But let it be determined to fight the battle and be assured that there is no better weapon than the cross.

Solid Foundations

It is important to understand that no one should expect to find great spiritual comforts in the first Mansions. This would be a poor way to build such a large and beautiful building. A foundation built on sand will collapse.[13] If we only receive blessings, then we can never be free from discouragement

---

[12] Judges 7:5
[13] Matthew 7:26-27

and temptation. For it is not in these first Mansions, but in those further on, that it rains manna.[14] When the soul arrives there, it has all that it desires, because it desires nothing but the will of God.

This is a curious thing. Here we are in this second Mansion, finding trials by the thousands. Our virtue is so young it has not yet learned to walk – in fact, it may not yet be born. And yet we expect spiritual favors during prayer and complain when we feel our spiritual life is dry.

This must not be true of you, sisters. Embrace the cross which your Spouse carried on His shoulders and realize that this cross is yours to carry, too. Find happiness in suffering for Christ's sake. If the Lord should grant blessings of spiritual favors, give Him heartfelt thanks, but this is not your primary concern.

You may think that you can only overcome spiritual trials if God gives you spiritual favors, but His Majesty knows best what we need. It is not for us to advise Him on how to treat us, for He has the right to tell us, "We know not what we ask."[15]

Remember, as this is very important, the only goal for the beginner in prayer is to overcome trials and resolve to do all they can to conform their will to the will of God. This is the greatest perfection that can be attained along the spiritual path. The more perfectly a person practices this, the more they will receive of the Lord and the greater the progress they

[14] Psalm 78:24
[15] Matthew 20:22

will make on this road.

Our entire welfare rests on doing the will of God, not following methods or mystical practices. We immediately go astray if we believe the Lord should do our will and lead us in the way we think is best. What kind of spiritual building can rest on this foundation?

Let us do our best to beware of the poisonous reptiles – these bad thoughts that come when God permits dry spells in our spiritual comforts. The Lord sometimes will even allow these reptiles to bite us so we can learn how to be on our guard in the future. And He may wish to see if we are disappointed when we offend Him.

Peace at Home

If you occasionally lapse into sin, do not lose heart or stop striving to make progress. For God can draw out good from your failure, just as a man drinks poison to prove the power of the antidote. If nothing else, failure reveals the torment within you and the harm of surrendering to sin.

Isn't the greatest evil being ill at ease in our own home? What peace can we hope to find if we have none within ourselves? And isn't our soul always in our company, like a relative or intimate friend who never leaves? Yet because of our sinful choices it feels like there is a war within us.

"Peace, peace," says the Lord.[16] My sisters, many times He spoke words of peace to His apostles. Believe me, unless we have peace, and strive for peace in our own home, we will not

---

[16] Luke 24:36, John 20:19

find it anywhere.

Let this war be ended. By the blood that Christ shed for us, I beg those who have not yet entered the Castle to stop this warfare. And I beg those who have already entered to not let the combat turn them back. Realize going backward is worse than a single failure from moving forward, and it will lead to ruin.

Do not trust yourself but trust the mercy of God. And you will see how His Majesty can lead you deeper into the Castle toward safe ground where beasts can't harass or hurt you anymore. Ahead, the beasts will become objects of ridicule with no power over us. When we arrive there, even in this life, we can enjoy more good things then we could ever desire.

Prayer and Meditation in the Second Mansion

In other writings I have explained how to apply prayer and meditation when you suffer these torments from the devil. At the beginning apply this habit gently, not with strenuous effort. In time, you will be able to practice the habit for longer periods of time.

Consult people of experience if you feel you are failing. Provided you do not give up, God will honor your efforts even if you find no one to teach you. The only remedy for giving up on prayer is to begin it again, otherwise the soul will start losing the battle. God grant that it becomes aware of its danger.

Some of you might suppose that if turning back is such a bad thing, it might be better to never enter the Castle at all.

But I told you at the beginning – and the Lord Himself says this – he who walks into danger perishes in it, and that the door to enter this Castle is prayer.[17]

It is absurd to think that we can enter heaven without first entering our own souls, coming to know ourselves, reflecting on our wretchedness and what we owe God, and continually begging His mercy. The Lord Himself says: "No one will ascend to My Father, but through Me," and "Whoever sees Me sees My Father."[18]

In this Mansion, to know Him we must look at Him and think of what we owe Him for the death He suffered for our sakes. If we never look at Him, I do not see how we can know Him or do works in His service. What value is there in faith without works? And what is the value of works that are not joined with the merits of Jesus Christ, our Good? And doesn't just the thought of Him awaken us to love Him?

May it please His Majesty to help us understand how much we cost Him, and how the servant is not greater than his Master.[19] Help us understand we must work to enjoy His glory. And we need to pray for this understanding, so we are not always entering into temptation.[20]

---

[17] Ecclesiasticus 3:26
[18] John 14:6, John 14:9
[19] Matthew 10:24
[20] Matthew 26:41

The Third Mansion

One

Spiritual Security

To those who by the mercy of God have won these battles and persevered to reach the third Mansion, what can we say but "Blessed is the man who fears the Lord"?[21] We certainly may call these souls blessed, for as far as we can tell, unless they turn back, they are on the safe road to salvation.

Here, sisters, you see how important it is to win the previous battles. I am convinced that the Lord gives the person who reaches this third Mansion a secure conscience, which is no small blessing. I say "secure," but remember, there is no security in life.

Understand that security only comes if you do not abandon the path you began on. It is a great misery to live with enemies always at our gates. We can't put down our weapons even to eat or sleep. We always fear enemies breaking through this fortress.

Oh, my Lord and my God! How can we bear such a miserable life? We wish You would put an end to it, unless there is hope of losing our life for You, spending it in Your service, or above all, discovering Your will for our life. If it is Your will, then may we die with You, as Saint Thomas said, for life without You and the fear of losing You is like death many times over.[22]

[21] Psalm 112:1
[22] John 11:16

That is why, my daughters, the security we should pray for is to one day dwell safely with the saints. What else could we hope for when our only pleasure is to please God?

Certainly, my daughters, I am fearful as I write this that I do not know what to say or how to continue. Ask His Majesty to always live within me, for otherwise what security can I feel after a life so imperfectly spent as mine? Do not be sad when you hear me talk this way. I know you like to think I am holy, and I would like to think so too. But I lost my holiness entirely through my own fault, not because God stopped helping me.

I am saying this with tears and shame because I realize I am asked to teach those who should be teaching me. What a hard task obedience has laid on me! May it please the Lord that this writing for Him be of some service to you. Ask Him to pardon this miserable and bold creature. His Majesty knows I have nothing to boast about but His mercy. I cannot cancel my past. There is nothing for me to do but approach God through the merits of His Son and His Virgin Mother, whose uniform you and I unworthily wear.

Praise Him, my daughters, for making you the daughters of our Lady. Do not be ashamed by my misery when you have such a good mother. Imitate her and consider her grandeur. It is a good thing she is our patroness, because even my sins and character can't tarnish our sacred order.

But I warn you, even though you are in this order and have such a mother, do not feel secure. David was a holy man, but you know what his son Solomon became. Do not rely on your separated life or that you are always talking about God, engaged in prayer, and withdrawn from desiring the things of the world – even if you view those things as worthless. That is all good, but as I have said, it is not enough to justify security. Meditate on this often: "Blessed is the man who fears the Lord."[23]

Lessons from the Rich Young Ruler

I do not remember what I was speaking about. I have digressed, and when I think about myself, I can't soar to think about higher things. I feel like a bird with broken wings. So, I will leave all this for now and return to what I began explaining concerning the souls that enter the third Mansion.

In enabling these souls to overcome difficulties in the first Mansions, the Lord has granted them a very great favor. Thanks to His mercy, I believe there are many such souls in the world. They never want to offend His Majesty and they avoid doing anything to disappoint Him. They love making up for wrongs done to others and spend hours in meditation. They use their time well, practicing works of charity to their neighbors, and are careful in their speech and dress. If they have a household, they govern it well.

The third Mansion certainly is a wonderful place to be. It seems there is no reason souls who have come this far should be denied entrance to the final Mansions. And the Lord will never deny entrance if they desire it, for this desire is an excellent way to prepare oneself so that every favor may be granted.

---

[23] Psalm 112:1

Oh, Jesus! Why would anyone in the third Mansion not desire to go deeper in the Castle, since they have overcome the most difficult part of the journey? Surely, everyone would want to continue.

But while many say they want this, in order to continue, the Lord must take complete possession of their souls. It is not enough just to say we desire to move ahead. The rich young ruler told Jesus he desired to follow Him, but he could not surrender all that he had.[24] I have been thinking a lot about that rich young ruler, for we are exactly like him.

Humility in Spiritual Dryness

Refusing to surrender our will is one reason our spiritual life can become dry, although there are many other reasons. When I talk about "spiritual dryness," I am not talking about difficult internal struggles that many good souls undergo, from which the Lord always provides a rescue. Internal suffering can come from no fault of our own, but great profit results from enduring it.

And when I talk about spiritual dryness, I am not referring to people who suffer from depression or other illnesses. In these cases, and all others, God is the judge. Usually, however, holding on to our will and not surrendering it to God is the cause for our spiritual dryness.

Souls in the third Mansion rarely sin intentionally. They make good use of their lives and their possessions. So, those who want to travel deeper in the Castle are not patient when

---

[24] Matthew 19:16-22

the door is closed to them. They are not willing to endure periods of spiritual dryness during which they – His servants – are excluded from the presence of the King. Yet on earth, a king has many servants, and they do not all get to enter his chamber.

Enter within yourselves, my daughters. Recognize your petty good works are the minimum expectation for a Christian. It is enough that you are a servant of God. Do not desire so much that the result is that you get nothing.

Look at the saints who have entered the King's chamber and you will see the difference between us and them. Do not ask for what you do not deserve. For no matter how faithfully we serve Him, we offend God when we think we deserve anything.

Oh, humility, humility! I do not know why I have this temptation, but whenever I hear people complain about their spiritual dryness, I can't help thinking they lack humility. Again, I am not referring to severe interior struggles, for this spiritual dryness is not due to lack of devotion. Let us test ourselves, my sisters, or allow the Lord to test us. For He knows what we need to learn, even though we often refuse His teaching.

And now let us return to these carefully ordered souls in the third Mansion and consider what they do for God. We shall see how wrong we are to complain to His Majesty. For if He tells us what we must do to progress, and we turn our backs and go away sorrowfully like the rich young ruler in the Gospel, what do you expect His Majesty to do?

God gives a reward in proportion to the love we have for

Him. And our love for Him can't just be in our heads, it must be proven by our works. Yet remember God does not need our works. What He wants is the strength of our wills.

It may seem to us that we who wear the religious habit have already shown strength of will by leaving behind the things of the world and all our possessions for His sake. Like Saint Peter, we may have only left our nets, but whatever we left seemed like a lot.[25] This is a good start. If we persevere in this poverty and detachment and stay away from the reptiles in the first Mansions, we will keep progressing deeper.

But I am warning you, even in demonstrating the strength of our wills we must consider ourselves useless servants. For, as we are told by Saint Paul and by Christ, realize that our Lord does not owe us anything.[26] Rather, the more we receive, the greater our debt.[27]

What can we possibly do for so generous a God who created us, gave us life, and died for us? Shouldn't we feel fortunate to repay something of what we owe Him by surrendering ourselves? This is the truth: For all the time He lived in the world He did nothing but serve. How can we ask for more gifts and favors?

Consider carefully, daughters, what I am saying. I can't explain it better; perhaps the Lord will make it clearer. May humility come from these periods of spiritual dryness. Do not let spiritual dryness cause you discontent, which is the aim of the devil. Know that where there is true humility, the Lord

---

[25] Matthew 4:20, Matthew 19:27
[26] Luke 17:10
[27] Luke 12:48

will give you peace and acceptance, even if not spiritual favors.

And the peace He gives will be enough. Sometimes God will give spiritual favors to those with weaker souls. But if we have the strength to walk in times of spiritual dryness, I think we would not want to exchange this for consolations. Test us, Lord – for You know the truth – so that we may know ourselves.

Two

Trials of the Well-Ordered Life

I know a few souls – perhaps a great many – who reached this third Mansion and lived an upright and carefully ordered life, both of body and mind (as far as one could tell). And then, after many years, when they were deluded into thinking they had become masters over their world, His Majesty sent them minor trials.

These poor people were so disturbed and disheartened by these trials that I became concerned for them. But it was useless to give them advice. Since they had practiced virtue for so long and believed they should be teaching others, they felt justified in feeling miserable. I never found any way of comforting or curing such people, except to tell them that I was sorry for their troubles.

When I see how unhappy they are, I really do feel compassion. They are convinced they suffer for God's sake, and it is useless to argue with them. They can't understand that their suffering is due to their own imperfection. This is the error of people who believe they are "advanced" in this third Mansion.

God, wishing for His people to realize their limitations, may temporarily withdraw His favor. In these trials, it does not take long for us to see ourselves for who we are without Him. When we finally realize the purpose of the trials, we better understand our shortcomings – and this may cause us more grief than the trials themselves. It is a great mercy from God that He teaches us this way. As we see our defects, we gain humility.

But there are some people who will not learn this way. They think their conduct is saintly, and they want others to think so, too. I will tell you about some of them so that we can test ourselves before we are tested by the Lord. It would be an advantage for us to know ourselves ahead of time and to prepare for the test.

A rich man with no children has no one to inherit his fortune. He happens to lose part of his wealth, but not so much that he should be concerned about the future. He still has enough for his household and some to spare. But if this loss causes him to worry as though he only owned a crust of bread, it reveals that he never released his money to the Lord's will. He makes an excuse for his anxiety by saying he is upset because he now has less money to leave to the poor. But God's desire is for the man to conform to His will, not for him to be charitable. This man should realize he lacks freedom of spirit and should beg the Lord to give it to him.

Another person who already has plenty of money sees an opportunity to acquire more property. If the opportunity comes to him, he should take it. But what if he strives for wealth, and after he gains it, he strives for more and more? No matter how good his intentions (and as I have said, people in the third Mansion have practiced virtue for a long time), he will never progress to the Mansions closest to the King.

It is the same for people in the third Mansion who are disrespected or whose reputation becomes damaged. God often grants them the grace to bear it well, for He loves to help people be virtuous in the presence of others. But some people are so disturbed by these incidents that they can't let them go. God help me! Are these not the same people who meditated on the pains our Lord endured and thought what a good thing it would be to suffer with Him? Yet they expect their life to always be well-ordered. Let us hope they do not imagine that their trouble is also someone else's fault.

You will think, sisters, that I am wandering from the point, and I am not saying anything that pertains to you. Yes, it is true that we own no property and that we are respected. These examples are not exactly applicable to us, but we can gain something from them. They demonstrate people who, despite their spiritual progress, have not left behind their desire for wealth and reputation. Through them you can test if you have truly abandoned what you say you have left behind.

Things happen that test our mastery over our passions. And believe me, it does not matter that we wear a religious uniform. It only matters if we strive to practice virtue and surrender our wills to God in everything, bringing our lives into accordance with what His Majesty ordains. Our desire should be for His will to be done, not ours.[28]

As we work on this, let us practice humility. Humility is the ointment for our wounds. If we are truly humble, God, the Physician, will heal us when He chooses.

---

[28] Luke 22:42

Travel Deeper

The service for God done by those in the third Mansion is as carefully ordered as their lives. They desire to serve God, but they are very careful to pick ways to serve Him which keep them safe. You never need fear that harm will come to them in God's service, for they are very reasonable people! Their love is not yet big enough to overcome their reason.

How I wish our reason would make us dissatisfied with the habit of serving God at a snail's pace! So long as we do this, we can't finish this journey to deeper Mansions. We seem to be constantly walking in fatigue – for believe me, this is an exhausting road. We are lucky if we do not get lost.

If it takes only one week to travel to another country, do you think, daughters, that we should make the journey over a year on bad roads through wind, snow, and floods? Wouldn't it be better to get the journey over and done with? We could avoid all the detours and danger of serpents. I could tell you a lot about that! Thank God I have traveled further, although sometimes I think I have not.

When we travel with all this caution, we find stumbling blocks everywhere. We are afraid of everything, so we do not dare go further. We think we can travel to deeper Mansions by letting others make the journey for us! This is not possible, my sisters.

So, for the love of the Lord, let us make real effort. Let us leave our reason and fears in His hands. Let us forget the weakness of our natures, which tends to make us anxious. Our task is only to journey with good speed so that we may be closer to the Lord.

Even though we have few or no comforts here, we are making a great mistake if we worry about our health, and worry won't improve it anyway. This I know. And I know that our spiritual progress has nothing to do with the body.

We may think we are moving forward, but in humility we should never suggest to others that we are spiritually advanced. The journey to the center of the Castle demands great humility, and lack of humility prevents our progress. When humility is present, the third Mansion is a most excellent place to be. If we do not have humility, we will stay here for the rest of our lives – burdened with a thousand afflictions and miseries.

If we can't abandon ourselves, the third Mansion will be difficult and oppressive. We will be weighed down by the mud of our miserable human natures, which is never carried by those who reach the final Mansions.

Spiritual Favors in the Third Mansion

In the third Mansion, the Lord never fails to repay our services. In His mercy, He gives us far more consolation than we deserve. He gives us greater happiness than we can find in earthly comforts or pleasures. But to prepare us to go deeper, I think in this Mansion He grants only enough spiritual delight to give us a taste of what may be ahead.

You will think that consolations and spiritual delights are the same thing, so why I am using different names? To me, they are very different, although I might be wrong. I will explain what I understand when we reach the Fourth Mansion, since I will have to explain the spiritual delights that the Lord gives there. I think when you understand the nature of each one, you will strive to pursue the one that is better.

Learning about the spiritual favors ahead will comfort souls whom God has brought thus far. But it will confuse those who think they have already achieved everything. If they are humble, they will be moved to give thanks. Those who are not humble will feel some inner shame they can't explain. For our reward is not to reach these spiritual delights but to have greater love and an increase in our actions of justice and truth.

You may wonder that if these spiritual favors are true – and they are – why teach about them? I do not know. You must ask my superiors who commanded me to write this, for it is not right for me to argue with them.

What I can truthfully tell you is that at one time I only read about these spiritual favors in books. I had no personal experience with them and never expected to in my life. Yet I praised God that He would grant these favors to souls that serve Him. It was happiness enough for me to know or hope I was pleasing to God in any way.

Now if my soul, which is so wretched, does this, then surely those who are good and humble will praise Him even more for the gift of spiritual favors. Even if a single person praises Him only once for His kindness in giving these favors, then this writing will be worth it. We should realize it is our own fault if we lose this pleasure and delight.

Moreover, if these favors come from God, then they come overflowing with love and strength for the journey. With their help, a soul can progress with less labor and grow in good works and virtue.

But remember, the Lord knows what you need. If He denies you these spiritual favors, the Lord is just and will provide for you in other ways.[29] His Majesty's secrets are hidden from us, but we can trust that all He does is best for us.

Spiritual Guides

Souls who by God's mercy have made it to the third Mansion (which is no small mercy, for they likely will progress further), will benefit from practicing prompt obedience. Even if they are not part of a religious order, it would be good for these souls to find a spiritual guide. These are people who can help them discern God's will so they might not follow their own will in anything. For this is usually how we do ourselves harm.

The person they choose should not be cast in the same mold as themselves. They should be people who act, rather than those who are only introspective. They should be detached from the illusions of the world, for in order to know ourselves, it helps to find someone who knows the world for what it is.

It is also a great encouragement to find a spiritual guide who easily does things we think are impossible. It makes us hopeful that we could fly someday. Seeing their flight makes us try to soar, in the way a young bird is taught by its parents. We are not ready for great flights, but we can learn by imitation. Receiving this help provides a great advantage.

---

[29] Psalm 119:137

Flee Temptation and Judgment

Souls in the third Mansion may feel they are strong enough to overcome temptation, but they should not trust their strength and expose themselves to danger. They are still so near the first Mansions that they might easily turn back.

The strength of souls in the third Mansion is not planted on the solid ground of those in deeper Mansions who are practiced in suffering. Those souls are familiar with the storms of the world and do not fear them anymore. And they do not find allure in worldly pleasures that could entrap a beginner.

But for those who have progressed only to the third Mansion, temptations may lead them to return to the temporary pleasures of the world. Be aware of this danger – you may be pressing ahead with great enthusiasm, trying to protect others from sin, and yet be unable to resist your own temptations.

Let us look at our own faults and not those of others. Those who live the carefully ordered lives of the third Mansion tend to be shocked by everything, but we could be learning important lessons from the people who shock us. Our outward behavior may be better than theirs, but even though this is good, this is not important. There is no reason we should expect others to make the same choices we do.

And we should not instruct others on spirituality when perhaps they do not even know what such a thing is. Even if God gives us a desire to help others, we can make many mistakes. It is best for us to live in silence and hope that the

Lord will take care of these wandering souls.[30] If we beg His Majesty to do so, His grace is their best help. May He be forever blessed!

---

[30] Isaiah 30:15

The Fourth Mansion

One

Before I begin, it is necessary for me again to give myself to the Holy Spirit and beg Him to speak for me so you can understand the Mansions ahead. For now we begin to touch the supernatural. Explanations will be difficult unless His Majesty takes them in hand.

He did this for me fourteen years ago when I wrote what was then the extent of my knowledge. Although I now have more to share, explaining what I know will be difficult. May His Majesty help me if there is any advantage to be gained from what I share, but not otherwise.

As these Mansions are nearer to the place where the King dwells, they are of great beauty. Many exquisite things are to be seen and appreciated in them, but they are delicate and difficult to explain. Anyone with personal experience, especially if they have a lot of it, will understand the spiritual favors in this Mansion very well. Without personal experience, those favors may seem obscure.

You might think that to reach these Mansions, one must live for a long time in the earlier Mansions. But there are no such rules, and this is not always the case. As you know, the Lord gives when He wills, as He wills, and to whom He wills. His gifts are His to give, and His choices are never wrong.[31]

In these next Mansions poisonous creatures seldom enter, and if they do, they are quite harmless. In fact, they can do the soul good because they reveal our weaknesses. It is also

---

[31] Matthew 20:15

better at this stage that the devil stays occupied with the poisonous creatures making war on the soul. If he wasn't busy with these temptations, he might do more damage interfering in the spiritual favors God may give us in this Mansion, since we have less experience with the supernatural.

Consolations and Spiritual Delights

As promised, I will describe the difference between the *consolations* and *spiritual delights* that we may receive in the fourth Mansion.

Consolations originate mainly from our own effort – although of course God has a hand in them because as in everything, we can do nothing without Him.[32] Consolations are the comforts we receive from our meditations, prayers and acts of virtue performed for our Lord.

We should feel good about our diligent spiritual devotion, which can lead to consolations. But understand that since consolations originate from our own effort, they are very similar to the joyful consolations we experience when good things happen to us on earth.

For example, let us say you inherit a large fortune, run into a person you dearly love, or are publicly celebrated for your success in an important business matter. Or perhaps you see your husband, brother, or son alive after you were told they were dead. I have seen people cry tears of joy from good things such as these, and in fact, I have done so myself. This joy comes from something good that happens to us or our

---

[32] John 15:5

accomplishments. This is why I believe earthly and spiritual consolations are similar, although of course consolations from spiritual devotion are nobler.

To sum it up, consolations from spiritual devotions begin in our human effort and end in God. Spiritual delights, on the other hand, begin in God and result in far deeper joy within us. How I wish I could make myself clear! I know the difference between these two joys, but I do not have the skill to make myself understood. May the Lord explain it for me!

I just remembered a verse we say at the end of the last psalm in our morning devotions. The last words of the verse are "for You will enlarge my heart."[33] If you have experience with consolations and spiritual delights, this verse is sufficient to explain the difference between the two. Consolations do not enlarge our heart – as a rule, they narrow it somewhat. The soul is happy for what it is doing for God's sake, but because consolations require our effort, it can feel like a burden that must be lifted continually.

Consolations may create strong emotions and we may shed tears of sorrow or joy from them, but perhaps this has more to do with the emotions of the soul. I wish I understood what comes from our soul and what comes from our human nature. If only I knew how to explain this, but my knowledge and learning come only from my experience.

In my own experience of consolations, I was so overcome by my meditation on the Passion of Christ that I wept until I had a severe headache. The same thing happens when I weep

---

[33] Psalm 119:32

over my sins. God gives me a blessing in these experiences. I won't say which of the two is better, but I wish I understood how they are different. My nature and temperament may cause me to cry, but as I have said, the results of these devotions are consolations from God.

Consolations should be treasured with humility. Having these experiences does not make us more deserving or spiritual. We do not really know if all these feelings come from our love for God. When they do, the gift is God's.

For the most part, souls in the previous Mansions are familiar with these joyful consolations resulting from the effort of our spiritual devotions. These souls work mainly with their intellect and reason, engaging in meditation. This is good for them, and they have not yet received the grace to do more. However, they would do well if they spent short amounts of time in other practices such as praising God, rejoicing in His goodness and in who He is, and desiring His honor and glory. They should do this as best they can because these acts awaken the will. When God gives the desire for these practices, they should be careful not to set them aside just to finish their usual meditation.

As I have written about this before, I won't repeat myself. I just want to warn you that to make quick progress and ascend into deeper Mansions, it is important not to think much, but to love much, so do what best stirs you to love God.

Perhaps we do not know what it means to love God. Our love for God is not measured by how delighted we feel about Him. We love God in the firmness of our determination to please Him in everything, in the size of our effort to avoid offending Him, and in how much we pray for Him to advance the honor and glory of His Son and the Church. This is true love for God.

Our Wandering Mind

Our love for God also is not measured by how much we can concentrate on Him during prayer, so if your mind becomes a little distracted you should not feel all is lost. I also struggle with a distracted mind. It was only about four years ago that I came to understand by experience that our mind and thoughts (or imagination) are not the same as our intellect.

The intellect is one of the faculties of the soul. I asked a theologian about this, and he said I was correct, which gave me great comfort. I could not understand how the intellect can be so steady while the mind can fly away so fast. It puzzled me that the faculties of my soul (my intellect) could be occupied and focused on God, and at the same time my mind could be confused and wandering. Only God can hold down the mind in a way that makes it feel separated from our body.

Oh Lord, have mercy on all that we suffer on this road through our lack of self-knowledge! The trouble is, we think we only need to learn about You and not ourselves. Even if we have wise people to consult, we do not always know what to ask. So instead, we suffer terrible trials because we do not understand ourselves. We worry about things we think are bad when they are not bad at all. In fact, they are good.

This lack of self-knowledge causes many people to

struggle with prayer. They become depressed and may even abandon prayer altogether. If only they could understand their interior worlds and how their minds and intellects work.

Just as the heavens revolve around us at high speed, so does our mind and imagination. And when our mind moves, we send all the faculties of the soul – our intellect – after it. We think that because our mind got lost, our time in prayer in the presence of God is wasted.

Yet while our mind has been running outside the Castle suffering the attacks of wild and poisonous creatures, our intellect was completely united with Him in the Mansion very close to the center near His presence.

Our time in prayer is worth the suffering of our mind, so a wandering mind should not upset us. And we should not abandon prayer, as the devil is trying to make us do. Our trials and worry come from the fact that we do not understand ourselves.

As I write this, the ringing in my ears I suffer from is so loud I am beginning to wonder what is going on inside. The noise makes it almost impossible for me to obey those who commanded me to write. My head sounds like it is filled with an overflowing river. As the river suddenly rushes downward, a host of whistling birds enters the top of my head. I have often thought that the highest part of our soul is at the top of our head, for the Spirit seems to move there. I hope I remember to write about this in the later Mansions.

I would not be surprised if God gave me this trouble in my head just so I could better understand these topics. Because despite all the turmoil in my head, it is not a hinderance to my prayers or to what I am saying now. The tranquility, love, desire, and clear knowledge in my soul are unaffected.

But how can my soul be undisturbed if it resides in the upper part of my head, which is filled with noise? That I do not know, but my experience says it is true. Somehow in prayer the faculties of the soul are suspended and at peace. It would be a terrible thing if these noises in my head forced me to give up prayer.

So do not worry about your wandering mind in the slightest. If the devil is responsible, he will eventually stop when our soul is suspended during prayer. Since our wandering mind comes from our weakness, let us have patience with ourselves and bear everything for the love of God. We are human. Just like we must eat and sleep because we are human, we also have other weaknesses that are best just accepted.

Let us admit our weaknesses in these areas and go where no one will despise us, as the bride says in the Song of Solomon.[34] I believe these words are properly applied here, for the shame of our interior battles is among the greatest trials we bear in life.

As I have said, we can bear any difficulty if we have peace where we live. If the Lord gives us rest from a thousand difficulties, but the cause of our trouble is within ourselves, it can be unbearable. So, Lord bring us to the place where these miseries will not taunt us, for they seem to be making fun of our soul. Even during this life, the Lord can free us from these

---

[34] Song of Solomon 8:1

miseries when we reach the last Mansion.

These weaknesses will not give everyone the same trouble or attack everyone as violently. For many years they troubled and attacked me. But I was hard on myself and felt I had to punish myself. Since it was painful for me, it might be for you. Therefore, I describe it in many ways hoping I can help you understand that our weakness is unavoidable, and you should not be discouraged or ashamed. Our mind is like an old mill that must keep going round and round to grind the flour. Let it continue to grind while we pay more attention to developing the faculties of our soul.

Sometimes our distractions will be worse and sometimes better, perhaps because of our health or age. The poor soul should not be blamed for this, although it will suffer. We are so ignorant about ourselves that I thought you would be comforted by the time I have spent explaining this. It is necessary – and His Majesty's will – that we learn to understand ourselves, and not blame our souls for the work of our weak imagination, our nature, or the devil.

Two

Two Bowls of Water

God help me in this task I have started. Business matters and my poor health forced me to set aside this work for a while. I can't read through what I have written, so I hope I can remember what I have already explained. I am afraid what I say will be confusing.

I previously explained consolations in the spiritual life, and how they are different from spiritual delights. Consolations come from the effort of our spiritual devotions and are sometimes mixed with emotion. They can cause us to weep and lose our breath. I have heard some people have nosebleeds or other upsetting physical effects, but I can't speak to this as it has not been my experience. But these experiences are still consoling in that they lead to a desire to please God and enjoy His presence.

In this fourth Mansion, the supernatural begins to touch the natural through spiritual delights. The experiences I refer to as a spiritual delight in God, or in other writings I have called the "prayer of quiet," are very different than consolations, as those of you who have experienced them by the mercy of God know.

To help you understand, let us imagine two large bowls filled with water. There are certain spiritual ideas that water explains for me, as I am ignorant, and my wits are no help. And, as I am fond of water, I have studied it more closely than anything else. In all the things our great and wise God has created, there are many valuable secrets, even in a thing as small as an ant.

These two large bowls you are imagining are filled with water in different ways. For one, the water comes from far away, through many noisy pipes designed by skilled workmen.

The other bowl, however, is built at the very source of the water. The flow of water into this second bowl is abundant, but it fills quietly. No machinery is required to fill this bowl and there is no need for the ongoing work of building pipes. The second bowl of water is always effortlessly flowing and overflowing.

In my opinion, the bowl and pipes built by men are like spiritual consolations. The water is sweet, but it only enters the bowl of our soul through our own efforts. For example, when we spend time meditating on creation, at last through our efforts comes satisfaction that fills our soul. But noise is made when the bowl needs replenishment again.

The second bowl obtains its water right from the source, which is God. When it is God's desire to give us a supernatural favor in the form of a spiritual delight, it comes to us like quiet water. We receive peace, calm, and sweetness from within ourselves. I can't say from where or how it comes.

When a spiritual delight arrives, we do not at first feel it in our heart, where earthly consolations are felt. The spiritual delight flows to every Mansion in our soul and into our faculties of intellect and reason. Finally, it overflows even into our body. That is why I say it begins in God and ends in ourselves. Anyone who has experienced this knows that the whole person – body, mind, and soul – are blessed by the experience of a spiritual delight.

I was thinking again about the verse that speaks of the heart's enlargement, "for You will enlarge my heart."[35] I do not think a spiritual delight arises from the heart but from a deeper interior place. And as I since have learned, I believe it arises from the center of the soul, which I will explain more about in the last Mansion.

I find secret things in myself that often amaze me. How many more secrets there must be! Oh, my Lord and my God, how wonderful You are! We go about here on earth like foolish shepherd boys who think they know You, but what we can possibly know amounts to almost nothing. There are profound secrets even in ourselves that we know nothing about. And though what we can know about You amounts to almost nothing, yet how great are the few mysteries we understand.

Spiritual Delights, or the Prayer of Quiet

Returning to this verse, "for You will enlarge my heart," I believe it can help us understand how heavenly water flows throughout us during these spiritual delights or the *prayer of quiet*. The water spreads within us and causes an interior expansion and indescribable blessing.

The soul does not understand what it is receiving. It is as if fragrant perfume was cast on an open flame in the depths of

---

[35] Psalm 119:32

our interior. We do not see the fire or where it comes from, but the fragrant smoke and heat penetrate the entire soul.

As I have said, the effects may extend to the body. Understand me, no heat is felt, no fragrance is detected. It is more delicate than this. I am only using this image to help you understand. People who have not experienced this must trust that it does happen. The soul understands this experience more clearly than my words can express.

It is not something imagined, because no matter how hard you try you can't work to acquire a spiritual delight. The very experience makes you realize that it is not of human metal but the purest gold of divine wisdom. I believe during a spiritual delight the faculties are detached from the experience of the soul and they watch fully amazed by what is happening. We become absorbed by the experience of a spiritual delight.

It may be that I am contradicting something I have said previously about this subject. It would not surprise me because in the fifteen years since I last wrote about it, the Lord has given me greater understanding. Both then and now I may be mistaken, but I can't lie about what I have experienced. By the mercy of God, I would rather die a thousand deaths. I speak of what I understand.

It seems clear to me that during the prayer of quiet, somehow our will is united with God's will. But it is important to use the best crucible to test the genuineness of the experience – how it affects our actions that follow. Our Lord gives a great favor if the person who receives the grace recognizes it for what it is and continues to press forward on the right path. The soul can't fully understand the favors the Lord grants us in these spiritual delights, or the love that draws us closer.

My daughters, I know you long to enter this state of prayer at once, and you are right in desiring this. I will tell you what I have learned about how to receive these favors. There are occasions when the Lord is pleased to grant these favors for no other reason than He wants to. He knows why He does it and it is not for us to interfere.

But setting this situation aside, practice what I have advised in the preceding Mansions: humility and more humility! It is by humility that the Lord allows Himself to be conquered. He will do all we ask of Him when we come with humility.

The first evidence of your humility is that you do not think you deserve these spiritual delights from the Lord, and you do not expect to receive them in your lifetime. You may ask, "But how can we gain them if we don't strive for them?" I reply that I have already described the surest way to obtain them – with humility.

There are many reasons why we should not strive for spiritual delights from the prayer of quiet.

The first reason is that we should love God with no motive or self-interest.

Second, we lack humility if we believe we deserve so great a reward in return for our miserable service.

Third, the preparation for receiving these gifts is a desire to imitate His suffering, not to receive His consolations, for we have often offended Him.

Fourth, His Majesty has not promised to give us these favors – He has promised us eternal glory if we keep His commandments. We do not need these special graces to be saved. He knows what is best for us and which of us love Him sincerely. I have known people who walk along the road of love only to serve our crucified Christ. Not only do they not ask for or desire spiritual delights, they beg not to receive any in this life.

Finally, any effort on our part to receive these spiritual delights is labor in vain. For this water does not flow through man-made pipes. We gain nothing by trying. No matter how much we practice meditation, deny ourselves or shed tears, we can't produce this water. Spiritual delights are only given to whom God wills and often when the soul is not thinking about them at all.

Sisters, we belong to Him. May He do with us as He wills and lead us wherever He pleases. I am sure if any of us achieves true humility and detachment, the Lord will grant us these favors and many others we can't even imagine. However, "true" humility and detachment are not only in our thoughts, for thoughts often deceive us. May He be forever praised and blessed! Amen.

Three

The Prayer of Recollection

I have explained the spiritual delights that can come from the prayer of quiet. But I want to say something about another kind of prayer I have explained in other writings, the *prayer of recollection*. Since I have taught about it elsewhere, I will only say a little.

The prayer of recollection brings our attention back to the presence of God in our soul. This prayer can lead to the prayer of quiet. To me, this prayer is supernatural because it is not dependent on our exterior condition. You do not need to be in the dark or have your eyes closed.

During the prayer of recollection, without effort you become alone in yourself. Gradually a temple is built inside of you from which you pray. All senses and external things seem to lose hold, while the soul recovers what it has lost.

Some say the soul enters within itself, and some say that it rises above itself. I have no skill in trying to explain this, but I will try to tell you what I know. I hope you can grasp my meaning, but perhaps I will be the only one who can understand myself.

Let us suppose our senses and faculties – the inhabitants of the Castle – leave the Castle for many days, which then turn into years. In their absence they become friends with enemies of the Castle. When our senses and faculties finally realize how much they have lost, they come back to the neighborhood of the Castle. They can't get back in through the main door because they have lost the habits that helped them enter.

But they are not traitors, and the great King of the Castle sees their desire to return. In His great mercy, He wants to bring them back from their wandering. Like a good Shepherd, He calls them so gently they barely hear Him, but they know His voice and return to the Mansions. So powerful is the Shepherd's call that it overcomes all that led them to wander.

I do not think I have ever explained the prayer of recollection as clearly before. When God grants the favor, He can be found readily within us. As Saint Augustine tells us, he finally found the Almighty within his own soul after having looked long for Him elsewhere.

But the prayer of recollection does not come from intellectual efforts or by imagining He is within us. While it is true that God is within us, and that this can be a good meditation to practice with the help of the Lord, the experience is more than just quieting the soul.

What I am explaining is quite different. As I have described, during the prayer of recollection people re-enter the Castle, but I can't say how they re-enter or hear their Shepherd's whistle. Some are already in the Castle but not thinking about God at all when they hear the Shepherd. In both cases, the call is not audible, but they become conscious of gently being drawn into themselves. And the soul recollects the presence of God within.

Anyone who has experienced this knows what I mean. Someone who knew what it felt like said it is like a hedgehog or tortoise withdrawing into itself. But these creatures enter within themselves whenever they want. For us, this experience happens not when we want it, but when God is pleased to give us this favor.

I believe His Majesty grants this favor of recollection to people who desire to surrender the things of the world, even if their state of life does not permit them to do so fully. For example, if you are married, you do not need to leave your marriage to be attentive to spiritual matters.

I also believe that if we desire to make room for His Majesty, He will give us not only this recollection of His presence in our soul but more as He leads us deeper into the Castle. Anyone who experiences this should give God praise. For it is a great favor and giving thanks will prepare us for even greater favors.

This recollection prepares us to listen to Him. Some books tell us that as we enter recollection, we should not try to use our reason but instead be aware of what the Lord is doing within our soul. But if His Majesty has not yet overwhelmed all our senses in a spiritual delight, then I can't understand how we can stop thinking.

This has been a matter of continual discussion among spiritual people, but I think there is no way of suspending our thinking without causing more harm than good. I confess my lack of humility, but their arguments were never good enough.

One person told me about a book by the saintly Fray Peter of Alcántara, and a saint I believe he is. He could have changed my mind, but upon reading it, I found he says exactly what I say with different words. He says, "Love must be awake."

It is possible I am mistaken, but I believe we should not suspend our thinking during recollection for the following reasons.

First, in this work of the spirit, a person does more if they desire less and think less of themselves. We should beg like a poor and needy person coming before a great and rich king, with eyes cast down, waiting humbly. When He gives secret signs showing He hears us, it is well for us to keep silent. In this case, there is no harm in suspending our intellect, provided we can do this. But if we are not sure if the King has heard or seen us, we should not stand there like a fool in silence, with our thoughts suspended. If we do this our soul is left dry and our imagination grows restless trying to stop thoughts. Instead, the Lord wishes us to remember we are in His presence and to call out for Him.

God knows what we need. In areas He limits, we should not apply human effort but leave action to Him. But there are many other areas where He does not limit our efforts, such as works of charity, prayer, and penance. With His help we can practice those for ourselves as far as our miserable natures are capable.

The second reason not to suspend our thinking during recollection is because what is happening inside of us is gentle and peaceful. Doing anything difficult would harm rather than help us. By "difficult" I mean forced – it would be difficult, for example, to hold our breath. Suspending our reasoning during the prayer of recollection would feel forced. The soul should leave itself in the hands of God, and do what He wills, resigning itself as much as possible without trying to gain an advantage.

A third reason is that the effort the soul is making to stop thinking will possibly awaken thought and cause it to think even more.

A fourth reason is that the most important and pleasing thing to God is that we remember His honor and glory, forgetting our benefit, comfort, and pleasure. If we are focused on trying to quiet our understanding and desires, how can we stop thinking about ourselves?

When His Majesty wants us to forget such things, He uses a different approach. He illuminates the soul's knowledge to such a high degree that we become so absorbed we lose control of our intellect. Without knowing how, we receive instruction better than any intellectual effort, since effort would only spoil everything. God gave us our faculties to work, so we should not try to cast a spell over them. They must be allowed to perform their duties until God determines a better approach.

As I understand it, the soul whom the Lord has been pleased to lead into this Mansion will do best to act as I have said. Without force or effort, we should strive to cut down the confusion of the intellect and maintain our understanding and thought. Let us remember Whose presence we enter.

If the prayer of recollection leads to spiritual delights during the prayer of quiet, that is good, but do not try to understand everything. This prayer is a gift bestowed upon the will. The soul should be left to enjoy this recollection and express its love, and it should not try to understand what is happening. Do not try to suspend your thoughts, although they may be suspended momentarily.

In talking about the experiences of the fourth Mansion, I talked about spiritual delights before the prayer of recollection. In fact, the prayer of recollection should have come first because it comes before the more intense and superior spiritual delights.

Recollection does not require us to give up the use of our mind and intellect. But in the prayer of quiet, the water comes right from the source. When this happens, the mind is confused and freezes, and then wanders everywhere in bewilderment. Meanwhile, the will is entirely united with God.

If you become distressed by your disturbed mind during the prayer of quiet, the soul loses the joy of the experience. You must forget about it and abandon yourself to the embrace of love during which His Majesty will teach the soul what to do next – mainly to be thankful and recognize its unworthiness to receive so great a good.

Effects of the Prayer of Quiet

I will go back to tell you about the effects of the prayer of quiet on the souls who receive this prayer from our Lord. An enlargement of the soul is apparent, as if the water coming from the spring has nowhere to go. Somehow the basin of our soul grows larger to accommodate the water that is pouring in. This is true of the prayer of quiet and other marvels God works in our soul that prepare and open it so it can be free to retain all He gives.

After His gentle touch, the soul is freer for service to God. It is not oppressed, for example, by the fear of hell, although it desires more than ever not to offend God. It no longer fears God like a servant fears their master, and it gains confidence that it will be with Him throughout eternity.

A person who limited their devotion now believes they are able to do all things through Christ.[36] The fear of future trials is diminished as their faith comes alive. They realize that all trials endured for God's sake will come with the grace to bear them patiently. Indeed, they even long for trials that arise from doing something for God.

As the soul better understands the greatness of God, it comes to realize the misery of its own condition. Having tasted spiritual delight from God, it recognizes the filth of earthly pleasures. Little by little, the soul withdraws from them, and in this way becomes more and more its own master. The soul is strengthened on the path toward virtue.

These effects do not occur because God once or twice grants the soul these spiritual favors. Spiritual nourishment must be received continually, for the welfare of the soul depends on frequent sustenance. With ongoing nourishment, the soul likely will continue deeper in the Castle unless it turns back at this point. For it does not matter how high one has climbed toward the summit – you lose everything when you turn back.

---

[36] Philippians 4:13

Warnings

I urge those who have reached this Mansion to avoid occasions of offending God. In this Mansion, the soul is growing in virtue and strength. It is not yet weaned – it is very much like a child beginning to nurse from its mother. If it is taken from its mother at this point it will die. I am afraid this is what can happen to those who give up on prayer at this stage. Unless they do so for some special reason or return to it soon, they will go quickly from bad to worse.

I know there is a great deal to fear in this matter as I have seen firsthand what can happen, and it has broken my heart. They leave Him who in His love was yearning to be their friend and had proven His friendship. I warn you not to engage in sin, because the devil would rather gain one of these souls than gain many who have not yet experienced the favors of this Mansion. For these souls could be of great benefit to the Church and would likely bring down others if they fall. The devil sees that His Majesty is showing them special love, and this is enough to make him do anything to bring their ruin.

Souls in this Mansion suffer many attacks, and if they go astray, their fall is great. You sisters, so far as we know, are free from these dangers. May God free you from pride and self-admiration. The devil sometimes offers counterfeits of the spiritual graces I have been mentioning, which can be detected because they produce the opposite effects in us.

There is another danger I want to warn you about, although I have spoken about it elsewhere. I have seen this in people misled by their emotions, especially women since we tend to show more feeling. These people allow their health to fail over their severe prayers, vigils, and penances. When they experience some interior consolation in their weakened physical condition, they believe they are experiencing a spiritual sleep (a prayer more intense than the prayer of quiet). But what they experience is just the result of their physical exhaustion.

They abandon themselves to this "spiritual" condition and grow physically weaker. They get it into their heads that they are in "rapture," but I call it foolishness. They are just wasting their time and ruining their health. They feel nothing through their senses, nor do they feel anything concerning God.

One person remained in this state for eight hours and was cured when she was told she had to eat, sleep, and do less penance. Fortunately, there was someone who understood her, although she had unintentionally misled her spiritual advisor and other people (including herself). I believe the devil would go out of his way to gain these types of people, and he was beginning to make good progress on this one.

It must be understood that when a state of rapture or absorption really comes from God, there may be lifelessness in the interior and exterior. But there is never lifelessness in the soul. The soul finds itself near God and is moved with great feelings. The experience only lasts for a short while, although the soul may become absorbed again.

Yet the prayer of quiet (when not caused by physical weakness) does not overcome the body or produce a physical sensation. If your weakened physical condition is the cause, tell your superior and distract your thoughts as best you can.

Your superior should reduce the number of hours you pray and ensure you are sleeping and eating well until physical strength returns.

If you are so weak that this is not enough, it should be clear that God is not calling you to the contemplative life. But there is room in convents for all kinds of people. Those who need more activity should be kept busy with duties and not left too often in solitude, where their health can suffer. The Lord may be testing your love by seeing how you bear His absence, and after a while He may be pleased to restore physical strength. If He is not, then vocal prayer and obedience will bring more benefit than other practices.

There also may be some who are weak in intellect – I have known some – and they believe they see everything they imagine. This is very dangerous and perhaps we will mention it again later, but not here. For I have already written at great length about this fourth Mansion where the greatest number of souls enter.

In this Mansion the natural is united with the supernatural, and it is here the devil can do the most harm. In the Mansions ahead the Lord gives him fewer opportunities. May He be praised forever. Amen.

The Fifth Mansion

One

Oh, sisters! How can I ever tell you about the riches, treasures, and delights found in the fifth Mansion! It would be better not to try to explain the Mansions to come, since they are indescribable and beyond our ability to fully comprehend. No comparisons are available on earth to explain them – they are completely insufficient.

Send me light from heaven, my Lord, that I might enlighten Your servants, some of whom receive these joys, for they are busy pleasing You. And help them not be deceived by the devil transfigured into an angel of light.[37]

The Hidden Treasure

Although I said "some of whom" receive these joys, there are many who enter this fifth Mansion. Some may explore more rooms in this Mansion than others, but the majority will get inside. Only a few will experience certain rooms, but God is showing great mercy if they do more than reach the door. For though many are called, few are chosen.[38]

All of us who wear this habit of Carmel are called to prayer and contemplation. The principles of our order were passed down to us by the holy fathers of Mount Carmel who sought this treasure, this precious pearl of Christ. But while we embrace solitude and contempt for the world, few of us are prepared for the Lord to reveal His treasures.

[37] 2 Corinthians 11:14
[38] Matthew 22:14

If we are careful about our behavior and virtue, we are on the right path. But to arrive at this Mansion, we need to do a great deal more. We can't be careless in great or small things.

So, my sisters, since in these Mansions – to the extent possible – we can enjoy heaven on earth, be brave in begging the Lord for help so it won't be our fault if we do not progress. Let Him show us the road and give us strength in our souls to dig until we find this hidden treasure.[39] The truth is that this treasure is within us. I hope I can explain this to you if the Lord is pleased to give me knowledge.

I say, "strength in our souls" because if you are not blessed with bodily strength it makes no difference. He has made it possible for anyone to buy His riches. And He is content if we purchase them with only what we have.

Blessed be so great a God! But notice, daughters, that to gain this treasure you can't hold anything back. No matter if you have a little or a lot, He wants it all for Himself. And in proportion to what we have given, we will receive greater or lesser favors.

Prayer of Union

In this Mansion, our prayers attain union with Christ. I will describe the test of whether we have attained this union. Do not think that the prayer of union is a dreamlike condition, although the soul seems to be in a drowsy state, neither asleep nor fully awake. We are only fast asleep to the things of the world and to ourselves.

---

[39] Matthew 13:44

In the short time of the prayer of union, the soul is unconscious and does not have the power to think, even if it wants to. You can't try to suspend your mind or senses. The soul does not understand how or what it loves or desires. It has completely died to the world to live more fully in God.

This is a delightful death. To come closer to God, the soul withdraws from the body. I do not know if the soul still has enough life to breathe. As I think about it, I believe it does not, and if it breathes at all, it does so unconsciously. While this is happening, the intellect wants to understand what it is feeling, but it does not have the strength. It becomes so stunned that even if consciousness remains, hands and feet can't move.

Oh, the secrets of God! If I thought I could explain them, I would never grow tired trying to describe them to you. I do not even mind writing nonsense, if just occasionally I could write sense and we could give great praise to the Lord.

In the union with Christ which occurs in this Mansion, the soul is certain that it is not dreaming. But without a great deal of experience, it doubts what has just happened. It wonders if the whole thing was a favor of God, or instead their imagination or the devil transfigured into an angel of light. It is left with a thousand suspicions, which is good because even in this deeper Mansion, our natures can be deceived.

For even though there is less opportunity for poisonous creatures to enter, a few agile little lizards hide all over this Mansion. They can only poke their heads in, and although they can't harm us, they are a bother if we pay attention to them. The lizards are the little thoughts that come from our imagination. But however agile they are, they can't enter this prayer of union because no imagination, memory, or thought can be a barrier to this blessing.

I believe that if this prayer of union is indeed our soul's union with God, the devil can't harm us. His Majesty is so joined with the essence of our soul that the devil does not dare approach, nor does he even know about this secret. Since it is said that the devil does not understand our thoughts, then he certainly can't understand an experience in which God limits our ability to think.

Oh, what a great blessing it is to be in a state during which the accursed one can do nothing to hurt us! Great are the gains in the soul when God is working on it and neither we nor anyone else can stop Him. God loves to give and can give all that He wills!

I am afraid I may be confusing you by saying, "if this is indeed our soul's union with God," and suggesting that there are different kinds of unions. But of course there are! Even the devil has different ways of playing on our vanities and desires for earthly pleasure. But the devil does not give us delight and satisfaction in our souls, or peace and joy.

This union with God is above all earthly joys, delights, and satisfactions. You will learn from experience that it is unlike any other delight. I once said it is as different as feeling something on the rough skin of our body compared to feeling it in the marrow of our bones. I do not know a better way to explain the difference.

Authentic Prayers of Union

It seems to me that this explanation of the prayer of union is not enough for you. You are afraid you will be mistaken in identifying when you experience this union. In reality, what has been said is already enough for someone who has experienced this blessing. But I want to mention a sign that I think can help you identify if the favor came from God. His Majesty put it into my mind only today.

In difficult topics, even if I think I am right and speak the truth, I say, "it seems to me" because if mistaken, I am prepared to listen to men with more learning. For even if they have not experienced these things, God uses them to give light to His Church. God enlightens them so they can discern truth. If they are dedicated servants of God, they are never surprised by His greatness, and they know He can do more than they expect. And when these learned men are studying matters which have no explanation, they look in their books for similar experiences.

I have had a great deal of experience with some educated men and timid half-educated men whose shortcomings cost me dearly. In my opinion, anyone who believes God can't do more than we understand, and who thinks that He does not give His creatures spiritual favors, has closed the door to receiving these favors.

Sisters, do not let this be true of you. Believe that God can do more. Do not focus on whether people who receive His favors are good or bad. His Majesty already knows, and there is no reason for us to meddle. Rather, we should serve His Majesty with humility, simplicity of heart and with praise for

His works and wonders.

Let us return to the sign I mentioned that can help you be certain whether the union you have experienced is from God. During the prayer of union, God makes the soul a fool to better impress true wisdom upon it. While the soul is in the state of union with God, it can neither see nor understand. This condition is always short and seems shorter to the soul than it is.

During the prayer of union, God places Himself in the interior of the soul in such a way that when the soul returns to itself, it is certain that God was there. It may be years later, and God may never grant the favor again, but so firmly does the truth of the encounter remain that it can never be forgotten or doubted. The soul is certain. This certainty is one of the signs of an authentic prayer of union. And this is apart from the effects of the union, which I will speak about later.

But now, you say, how can the soul be certain when it cannot see or understand? I am not saying that the soul has certainty in the moment, but the soul has certainty afterward. It is certain not because of a vision but because of the certainty that remains in the soul, which can only be put there by God.

I know about a person who did not know that God is in all things by His presence, power, and essence. She only came to believe this when God granted her the favor of the prayer of union. When she asked one of those ill-instructed men I mentioned earlier, "In what way is God in us?", he told her God was not present in our souls but only present by grace. She was so certain about her experience that she did not believe him. It was a great consolation when others told her the truth.

Do not make a mistake by thinking this certainty has anything to do with seeing the bodily presence of our Lord Jesus Christ. This does not happen in the prayer of union. So how can we be convinced of something we do not see? I do not know – that is the work of God. But I know I am speaking the truth.

If anyone does not have this certainty impressed on their soul, then what they experienced was not a union of the whole soul with God. It might be a union with one of their faculties or some of the other favors God grants the soul. Since our intellects can't understand this union, we should stop trying. It is enough to know that He who is the cause of this is Almighty.

And we have no part in bringing this union about, no matter how hard we try. The bride in the Song of Solomon says, "The King brought me into the wine cellar."[40] Since she was wandering elsewhere looking for her Beloved, it is clear she did not go to the wine cellar herself.[41]

I understand our union with Christ to be the wine cellar in which He puts us when and as He wills. We can't enter by our own effort. His Majesty must put us in the very center of our soul, and He enters there Himself to show us His wonders. It is His pleasure that our surrendered will has no part in this.

And He also wants to keep the doors of our faculties and

---

[40] Song of Solomon 2:4
[41] Song of Solomon 3:2

senses closed, for they are asleep during the prayer of union. He enters into the center of our soul without going through any door, the same way He entered the place where the disciples gathered after His resurrection and said, "Peace be with you," and in the same way He left the tomb without removing the stone.[42] You will see in the final Mansion how His Majesty wants the soul to enjoy Him fully at its center, even more than in this Mansion.

Oh, daughters, how much we will see if we can give up our sinfulness and misery and understand we are not worthy to be His servants. We can't comprehend His marvels. May He be praised forever. Amen.

---

[42] John 20:19

Two

The Silkworm's Cocoon

You might think we are done describing this fifth Mansion, but there is much more to share. Regarding the nature of the union, I do not know that I can say more. But there are many more things to be said about the work the Lord does in us when we are prepared for the favor of the prayer of union. For while we can do nothing to make His Majesty grant us this favor, we can do a great deal to prepare ourselves for it.

To explain things better, I want to use a helpful comparison. You have heard of the wonderful way silk is made – a way only God could invent. The silkworm comes from eggs that look like tiny peppercorns. I have never seen them myself, but I am relying on what I have been told.

When the warm weather comes and the mulberry trees begin to leaf, silkworms emerge from the eggs. The silkworms feed on the mulberry leaves until they are fully grown and then settle upon twigs, where they begin spinning silk from their tiny mouths. The silk strands create a tight little cocoon in which they bury themselves, and finally, the ugly silkworm emerges as a beautiful white butterfly.

Now, if no one had ever seen this but had only heard about it in a story, who would believe it? How can we believe that the diligent work of a worm could produce silk? Or that the poor little worm would lose its life?

The Fifth Mansion

This alone is sufficient for a brief meditation on the wonders and wisdom of our God. What would happen in us if we understood the properties of everything created by God? It is beneficial to be busy thinking of these wonderful things and rejoicing that we are brides of such a wise and powerful King.

Let us return to the silkworm. The silkworm is like the soul that comes to life through the warmth of the Holy Spirit. It nourishes itself on the help that God gives all of us and the support He gives us through His Church. This includes meditation, confession, good books, and sermons necessary for a soul that is dead in sin and frequently plunged into temptation. The soul grows as it nourishes itself with this food.

What concerns us in this Mansion is what happens when the soul is fully grown. When the silkworm reaches maturity, it spins its silk to build the house in which it will die. The house may be understood to mean Christ, since I have read that our life is hidden in Christ, or that our life is Christ.[43]

Here then daughters, is how we can prepare ourselves – our home – for the prayer of union. May His Majesty Himself be the home that we construct for ourselves in which to hide. When I say, "He will be our home," I seem to suggest we can take God away or build Him up since I am describing Him as the home we are building. Of course, we can't possibly do that!

But we can build our cocoon by taking away from our *self*,

---

[43] Colossians 3:3-4

just as the silkworm produces silk from itself to build its cocoon. And God will take this tiny achievement of ours and unite it with His greatness. He will give this work such value that God Himself will be the reward. Since He paid the highest price, He unifies our small labors with the great ones He suffered.

Take courage, my daughters! Let us move quickly to the task of spinning this cocoon. Let us renounce our self-love and self-will, and our attachment to earthly things. Let us practice prayer, repentance, self-denial, obedience, and all the other good works that you know. Let us do what we have been taught.

Die! Die as the silkworm does when it completes the work it was created to do. Then, when we are completely hidden in His greatness like a little worm enveloped in its cocoon, we shall see God. When I say we shall "see God," it is the way we experience Him in this kind of union.

The Butterfly

Now let us see what happens to this silkworm after it is fully grown, for everything I have said leads up to this. After the soul is in this prayer of union, truly dead to the world in its cocoon, it emerges as a little white butterfly.

Oh, the greatness of God! How the soul is transformed after being hidden in the greatness of God! The close unity with Him is brief, never I think even half an hour. I tell you truly the soul does not even know itself – think of the difference between an ugly worm and a beautiful butterfly.

The soul does not understand how it could deserve such a

blessing, and it knows full well it does not deserve it at all. After it emerges, it finds itself anxious to praise the Lord and die a thousand deaths for His sake. It can't keep itself from longing to suffer great trials. It strongly desires spiritual disciplines, solitude and for everyone to know God. And from then on, it becomes greatly distressed when it sees God being offended.

In the next Mansion, many of these experiences are the same, but they come with greater power. For after God visits a soul on earth, it experiences great things as it strives to travel deeper into the Castle.

Despite that it is quieter and more peaceful than it has ever been before in its life, see the restlessness of this little butterfly! Here is something to praise God for – the butterfly does not know where to settle and make its home anymore. Everything on earth is now dissatisfying, especially when God again and again brings the wine of a new blessing. And the butterfly no longer values the work it did as a worm weaving its cocoon. It has wings now, so how can it be content to crawl when it can fly?

All that it can do for God seems small compared to what it wishes to do. It even dismisses what saints endure, knowing by experience how the Lord can help and transform a soul into something unrecognizably beautiful. The difficulty it used to have confessing and repenting from sin is now turned into a strength.

Its attachment to relatives, friends or wealth is gone and now it is pained to fulfill daily obligations. Before this transformation, the soul was powerless to these attachments despite all its will and resolution. Any effort only made the binds tighter. Everything now wearies this transformed soul because it knows no other creature can give it true rest.

While I have said a lot already, there is much more I could say. Anyone who has received this favor will realize I have said very little. It is not surprising that this little butterfly feels like a stranger on earth. It should find a new resting place, but where will it go? It can't return to the cocoon, for it is not in our power to go back unless God grants us this favor again.

Oh, Lord! What new trials begin for this soul! Who would think this would happen after it received such a favor? But we have crosses to bear one way or another for as long as we live.

If anyone says they experience continual peace and joy after reaching this Mansion, I do not believe they have arrived here yet. Or perhaps their experience is because of a natural weakness or maybe even the devil, who gives peace to a soul temporarily to wage a greater war upon it later.

I do not mean to say that those who experience the prayer of union no longer have peace. They do have deep peace, and even in trials they often experience peace and happiness. But discontentment with things of the world gives rise to the painful desire to leave the world.

The soul's only relief is the thought that God wants it to be living in this exile. If this does not provide comfort, then despite everything that has been gained, this reveals that the soul is still not fully resigned to God's will. It may be acting in conformity with God's will, but in tears and sorrow it knows it still lacks the grace to fully submit.

Every time the soul is in prayer, it feels the pain of this

regret. Perhaps this pain is also the result of seeing how often God is offended, how little He is esteemed in this world, and how many souls are lost. Its greatest pain may come from the possible condemnation of Christian souls who fall away, although God is great in mercy and no matter what they have done, they can repent and be saved.

Oh, the greatness of God! Only a few years ago – maybe only a few days ago – the soul was thinking only of itself. And now, how does it feel such anxiety for God's reputation and the salvation of others? Even years of meditation on how much sin offends Him, how those who are condemned are His lost children, and how good it would be to depart from this miserable and dangerous life, can't create the pain this soul feels now.

All those meditations do not produce the kind of grief I am talking about – the grief that reaches to the depths of our beings. This grief comes without any effort on the soul's part and even against our will. This grief will tear you to pieces and grind you to a powder.

God's Stamp on our Soul

I said earlier that in the Song of Solomon, the bride is brought to the wine cellar by God. While in the cellar, God wraps the banner of love over her.[44] This is what happens in the cocoon. The soul is delivered into His hands. His great love so completely overpowers the soul that it neither knows nor desires anything except for God to do with it as He wills.

---

[44] Song of Solomon 2:4

I think He only gives this favor to the soul that He takes for His very own. His will is that the soul, without knowing what is happening, is sealed with His seal. The soul is like wax softened for a stamp. The wax does not soften itself, but someone must prepare it to be sealed. It rests quiet and consenting. Oh goodness of God, all this must be done at a cost to You! You only require our will and ask that the wax does not resist.

So now you see, sisters, what our God does to a soul in the prayer of union so that they know they are His. He gives from what He has – which is what His Son received in His life on earth. He can give us no greater favor.

At the Last Supper, He was not thinking about the difficult death ahead of Him, or the approaching pain and fear. Who would have wanted to depart more from this life than Him in this moment?

Instead, His Majesty said, "I have eagerly desired to eat this Passover with you."[45] Why was this more important than the desire to escape His terrible death? His answer, "Because the great sorrows I suffered and continue to suffer are nothing compared to My great love and desire to save souls."

I have often thought about the anguish a person I know suffers when seeing the Lord offended. It is so intolerable to her that she would rather die. I have thought that since her soul has much less love than Christ – almost nothing in comparison – imagine the feelings of our Lord Jesus Christ. What a life of suffering He lived if He continually witnessed

---

[45] Luke 22:15

offenses committed against His Father.

I think this must have caused Him greater pain than the pains of His most sacred death. In His death He could see the end of His trials. He would be satisfied with the redemption achieved through His difficult death, proving His love and obedience to His Father. This thought would alleviate His pain, just as the strength of our love reduces our suffering in great trials and increases our wish for more.

How excellent it was for His Majesty to show His Father His complete obedience and love for His neighbor! Oh, the great delight of suffering to do the will of God! But I believe that only because He was God and man, He could endure one day witnessing the many offenses committed against His Majesty, and the many condemned souls.

Three

Let us return to our little dove and see some of what God gives her in this Mansion. Even if she has traveled this far into the Castle, she still must advance in self-knowledge and service to our Lord. If she receives the favor of union but begins leading a careless life and strays from the road to heaven (disregarding the commandments), she shares the fate of the creature who emerges from the silkworm. This creature produces eggs and then dies forever.

Despite what happens to this butterfly, God wills that the great favor of union produces fruit. Even if the soul does not profit from the spiritual favor given, other souls will. For since a soul is left with the desires and virtues previously mentioned, it will give off heat that causes others to catch fire. And even after the soul loses this heat, it still hopes others will benefit, and it delights in explaining the favors God grants to those who love and serve Him.

This happened to a person I know. After experiencing the prayer of union, she went far astray, but she still enjoyed helping others by teaching about the way of prayer and the spiritual favors God had shown her. Later, the Lord gave her new light.

But how many are called by the Lord to the communion of apostleship, as Judas was, or called to become a king, as Saul was, and then through their own fault, they go off course! From this, sisters, we conclude that to continue to progress and avoid straying like Judas or Saul, our only safety lies in obedience to following the law of God. And I am speaking here to everyone, whether you have received these favors or not.

Union through Submission

Despite everything I have said, this Mansion is difficult to understand. There is a great deal to be gained from entering. If the Lord withholds the supernatural gifts of the prayer of union, do not be disappointed. For true union also can be achieved with the blessing of our Lord if we try to keep our will fixed only on that which is God's will.

Oh, how many of us say we submit and believe we are only after God's will! We even say we are willing to die to prove it is true. If we are truly submitted to God's will, then I repeat, we have already obtained the grace of union with God. Indeed, you do not need to wish for the prayer of the union because you already have achieved its purpose – to resign your will for your life.

How joyful is this union! The happy soul that achieves this union lives peacefully in this world and the next. No earthly events can trouble it, except the danger of losing God or seeing Him offended. The soul is at peace even in sickness, poverty, or the loss of death – except the death of someone useful to the Church, but the soul knows God is wiser than our desires.

Understand there are many types of suffering. Some suffering comes upon us suddenly because of our human nature. Suffering may even come when we have compassion for our neighbors. The Lord suffered in this way before He raised Lazarus.[46] We suffer like this even if we are united with God's will, but this suffering no longer creates restless turbulence in our souls. It soon passes because like spiritual consolations in prayer, it only affects our senses and faculties, not the depths of our soul. And suffering does not enter the final Mansion.

The Lord has the power to provide many ways to enter this Mansion, and not just through the prayer of union, which seems like a shortcut. But to enter, be sure of this, my daughters: The silkworm must die. It is this that costs you the most. We must give our self the death blow.

Because you see your new life with God during the prayer of union, death comes more easily. In the other approach to union – submitting to the will of God – the work will be difficult, but the reward will be greater if you can overcome. There is no doubt this you can achieve a true union with the will of God through this approach. And this is the union that I begged all my life for our Lord to grant me, as it is certain and safe.

But how few of us obtain this union! Those who are careful not to offend God or who enter the religious order think they have done everything necessary to submit to God's will. But how many maggots remain hiding in us, destroying our virtue, just like the worm that ate Jonah's vine.[47]

These pests are self-love, self-esteem, rash judgment of others even in small things, and a lack of love for our neighbor

---

[46] John 11:33-36
[47] Jonah 4:6-7

– certainly not as much as we love ourselves. We may do everything to avoid sin, but not do enough to root out sin to obtain perfect union with the will of God.

What do you think God's will is, daughters? His will is that we should become holy and be one with Him and the Father, as in His Majesty's prayer.[48] Consider how far we are from achieving this. I am distressed as I write because I know through my own fault how far I am from God's will. We do not require great spiritual favors from our Lord to achieve His will. He has given us all we need and His Son to show the way.

Submitting to God's will does not mean that we will not have sorrow at the death of our father or brother, or that we must have joy in trials or sickness. The only virtue we can bring ourselves to in these times may be a positive attitude. Even philosophers have to lean into their own wisdom sometimes.

Our Lord asked only two things from us: to love Him and to love our neighbor.[49] This is what we should be working toward. If we are obedient to both these commands, then we are united with His will. But as I have said, we are very far from obeying and serving our Master perfectly in these two areas. May His Majesty give us the grace to reach this union, as it is within our power if we wish.

Love your Neighbor

I think the most important indication that we are keeping

---

[48] John 17:22
[49] Matthew 22:37-40

these two commandments is if we have a genuine love for others. It is hard for us to know how well we love God, even if we think we have strong evidence. But there can be no doubt about whether we love our neighbor.[50]

Certainly, as you increase your love for others, you increase your love for God. His Majesty loves us so much that I am sure He will repay our love for others by increasing our love for Him in a thousand different ways.

It is important for us to walk with careful attention to how we are loving our neighbor, for if we practice this perfectly, we have done everything. But because our nature is bad, we can never have perfect love for our neighbor if that love does not have its roots in the love of God.

Since this is so important, sisters, let us get to know every detail about ourselves better and better. Do not pay attention to the great works we plan during prayer that imagine wonders we perform for others or souls we save. These plans will never happen if we do not act, so why are you so certain you will do them?

The devil is cunning. He will run a thousand times around hell if by doing so he can make us believe we have humility or virtue. These delusions are very harmful. When we have imaginary virtue accompanied by vanity, they come from the devil. Plans that God gives are free from self-importance and pride.

I am amused when I see some people pray for God's sake to be humbled and openly shamed – and then do everything

---

[50] 1 John 4:20

they can to hide their small failures. And if they are accused of something they did not do, God help us from having to listen to them!

Let anyone who can't bear trials like this be careful about resolutions made in private. Resolutions should be made by the genuine act of your will, not by your imagination. The devil makes good use of our imagination in his lies, and practices on women and uneducated people who do not understand their interior life and the difference between their faculties and their imaginations.

Sisters, how clearly people see how much you love your neighbor, and how clearly they see when you do not! If you understood the importance of this virtue, you would strive after nothing else. I see how little people understand the road to union when I see them wrapped up in their prayers. They think this is what union is about.

But no, sisters, no. What the Lord wants is our work. If you help a sick woman, do not worry that you will have less time for prayer. Take pity on her. If she is in pain, feel her pain. If she is hungry, give her your food. Do not only do it for her sake but do it because you know it is the Lord's will.

This is true union with His will. If you hear someone being praised, be much happier than if they were praising you. This is easy if you have humility, for in that case you are sorry to hear yourself praised. It is a great thing to be glad when your sisters are praised, and to conceal their faults and feel sorrow for them as if they were your own.

Sisters, I know if we fail in the love of our neighbor all will be lost, so I have said a great deal about this. May the Lord help you succeed. For if you do not fail, then I am certain you will obtain the union we have been talking about. If you lack love for your neighbor, even if you think you attained a union with God through the prayer of union (for some think this is enough), I assure you that you have not.

Beg our Lord to give you perfect love for your neighbor and leave the rest to Him. He will give you far more than you desire if you discipline yourself and work with all your power. Force yourself to go along with your sister's wishes even if it means you must give something up. Forget your self-interests for theirs. However much your nature fights you, act on every opportunity to ease the burden of your neighbor.

Do not think that it will cost nothing, and all the work will be done for you. Think about the love He bore for us. To free us from death, He suffered the most painful death of all – death on the Cross.

Four

Y ou may be anxious about what happens to our little dove and where she finds rest, since she can't find it in spiritual delights or earthly consolations. Our little dove takes a higher flight, and until we come to the last Mansion, I can't give you the answer. May God grant me the time and memory to write about this. It has been nearly five months since I began this work. My head is too weak to reread it, so what I say may be repetitive or in the wrong order. Fortunately, this work is only for my sisters.

Spiritual Engagement

I want to explain more about the prayer of union and, to the best of my small wits, try to draw a comparison. Later we will talk more about the little butterfly, who is always doing good for itself and others because, since it can't find rest, it never stops.

You have often heard that God becomes spiritually engaged to souls. May He be praised for so utterly humbling Himself. I can't find a better comparison than the sacrament of matrimony, although the two are very different.

In this divine union, everything is spiritual, nothing is physical. It excels above human marriage a thousand times in mutual delight and the joys God gives. Love is joined with the Creator of love. It is so pure and sweet that it can't be described, but the Lord makes the soul deeply conscious of it.

In this Mansion, the union does not reach a spiritual marriage but is more like what happens when two people are deciding if they want to become engaged. They discuss whether they are suitable for one another and love each other. They spend time together to help make their decision to marry.

It is the same for this union with God. The soul agrees to the union as it understands the great advantages. It resolves to fulfill the will of the Spouse in all things and do all it can to please Him. His Majesty knows the truth of the soul's commitment and in return, wishes to bless His future bride. To help it know Him better, He gives it the favor of visiting and drawing the soul into His presence. We might compare the prayer of union to this.

These visits only last a little while. There is no longer any question that the marriage will proceed, but the soul wants to learn more about the Bridegroom it will marry.

Even in a thousand years, the senses and faculties could not gain the knowledge that is passed quickly in the prayer of union. The Spouse, being Who He is, in one visit leaves the soul more eager to join hands with Him. The soul becomes so full of love that it will do anything not to jeopardize this divine betrothal. But if the soul is neglectful and gives its affection to anything other than Himself, it loses everything. This is as great a loss as the favors given, which are precious beyond description.

Warnings

Oh, Christian souls whom God has brought this far! I beg

you for His sake not to grow careless. Avoid all occasions of sin. Until the marriage which takes place in the next Mansion, you are not strong enough to avoid temptation. In this Mansion, the engaged couple has only spent a little time together.

The devil will spare nothing to prevent the marriage. He only stops interfering after the bride surrenders in marriage, since the devil knows then that his interference only will build more goodness in the bride.

I tell you, daughters, I have known people advanced in spiritual life who reach this Mansion and fall to the devil's deceitful tricks. I have often said that all hell leagues together against such souls because Satan knows that the loss of just one results in the loss of many more.

We should praise God for how He can use one man to draw many to Himself. Think of the multitudes converted by martyrs or one young maiden, Saint Ursula! And how many victims the evil one was deprived of by Saint Dominic, Saint Francis, and other founders of religious orders. How many is the devil losing today through Father Ignatius, who founded the Society of Jesus!

When we read about their lives, we learn they received grace from God to accomplish great good. This was only possible because they made a great effort not to lose their spiritual engagement through their own fault.

Oh, my daughters, how willing our Lord is to grant us the same graces! And since there are fewer of us who care for His honor, there is an even more urgent need for people to receive such favors.

But we are deceived – we love ourselves too much and are too careful to keep control. May God in His mercy enlighten us so that we do not sink into darkness.

You may have two questions. First, if the soul is united with the will of God and following His pleasure, as I have explained, how can it ever be deceived? And second, how can the devil destroy our soul when it is withdrawn from the world and frequently nourished by the sacraments? How can the devil wreak havoc on us when we are in the company of angels (as we might say), and by God's mercy we only want to serve and please Him in everything?

It makes sense that people immersed in the cares of the world have a higher risk of straying. I believe you are right about this, and God grants us a great deal of mercy in our protected Order. But as I said earlier, Judas was among the apostles, and he was in the company of God Himself and heard His words – yet this did not make him safe.

To your first question, if the soul is always faithful to the will of God, it can't be lost. But the evil one schemes by presenting something that seems good. Little by little, he leads the soul astray on a trivial sin that it believes is harmless. Gradually, reason is compromised, and the will is weakened. The devil nurtures his victim's self-love, until slowly he succeeds in breaking the union with the will of God, and the soul soon follows its own will.

The answer to your first question answers your second question. No fence is strong enough to keep Satan out, and no desert is remote enough for him to avoid. And God may permit Satan to tempt a soul to prove its virtue. If God wants to use this soul to enlighten others, it is better for the soul to fail in the beginning than to fail later on, when it can cause more harm.

Constantly beg God to uphold us by His hand. The truth is, if He ever leaves us, we will certainly fall into the abyss. Never be so foolish as to trust in yourself.

After this, I think the greatest safeguard is to watch whether we advance or fall back in virtue. Especially monitor your love for your neighbor, your desire to be thought of as least of all, and how you perform ordinary, everyday duties. If we watch this carefully and beg our Lord to show us our faults, we should see if we are advancing or falling back.

But do not think that if the soul has gotten this far, God will abandon it easily to the schemes of the devil. When His Majesty sees a soul leaving Him, He feels the loss keenly. He will give the soul a thousand secret warnings about the hidden danger.

Go Deeper

Finally, while we have come far to reach the fifth Mansion, we must go deeper. As long as your love is active, it is impossible not to go deeper. Be concerned if you do not go further, for without a doubt the evil one is planning harm. Recognize danger if you find you are not growing in virtue. The one who is engaged to be the spouse of God Himself should not rest.

In the sixth Mansion I will show you, daughters, how Christ treats the souls He takes for His brides. You will see that the immense favors to come far surpass all that we do or suffer in preparation.

Perhaps our Lord wanted me to write this just so you would know about the great rewards to come and His infinite mercy to give Himself to worms like us. Only then maybe we would forget our wretched, petty, earthly pleasures and, ignited by love, run toward Him with our eyes fixed on His Majesty.

May He help me explain the difficult topics ahead, for if our Lord and the Holy Spirit do not guide my pen, the task will be impossible. I beg Him to only let me say what will be helpful to you. His Majesty knows that to the best of my ability, I only wish for His name to be glorified and to strive to serve a Lord who blesses our efforts even in this world. His favors on earth show us something of the joy we can expect in heaven.

And think how our future joy will be uninterrupted by the trials and dangers of this stormy sea of life. If it were not for the fear of losing Him or offending Him, we should wish to live until the end of the world so we could work in the service of our great God, Lord and Spouse. May His Majesty help us produce good works for Him, free from our faults. Amen!

The Sixth Mansion

One

With the help of the Holy Spirit, I present the sixth Mansion, where the soul is wounded with love for its Spouse. Now more than ever the soul yearns to be alone with Him as much as the duties of life permit. The soul who experienced the prayer of union in the fifth Mansion was so imprinted by the sight of Him that it only desires to meet Him again, although nothing was actually seen with eyes or imagination.

This soul is now determined to have no other spouse than our Lord. But He does not want a speedy engagement. He wants our longing to be stronger, and the blessing of our spiritual marriage to come at some cost. And while this cost is minimal compared with the great blessing, I assure you, the soul needs the promise of marriage to help it endure the delay.

Oh God help me, how many interior and exterior troubles we must suffer before we enter the seventh Mansion! Naturally weak as we are, I wonder if we would have the resolve to face these trials if we knew about them ahead of time. By the time we reach the seventh Mansion, we are prepared to fear nothing. From then on, we boldly suffer all things for God through the strength of our almost uninterrupted union with Him.

I think it will help you to understand the trials you may face in the sixth Mansion. It is possible that not all souls will be led this way, but I think those who enjoy heavenly favors can't be completely free of earthly troubles in one way or another. It will be a comfort for you to learn that God provides great favors when you feel everything is lost.

Suffering from False Criticism

I will not cover these trials in any certain order but as they come to my memory. I begin with the least severe: false criticism and gossip by people who doubt the authenticity of your faith. These people may know you well or not know you at all.

People who doubt your sincere faith may say things about you such as "She's pretending to be a saint" or "She's purposefully making good Christians who do not draw attention to their works look bad." But the truth is, you are just diligently going about your responsibilities. People who you thought were friends abandon you, making the most bitter remarks of all. "Her soul is ruined," they say, and "She is obviously being led astray doing the devil's work." Or they say, "She's going the way of so-and-so, who ruined their life and dragged good people down with them," or "She's deceiving her spiritual advisors." They even visit your spiritual advisor and make a thousand accusations against you, giving examples of others who fell into ruin this way.

I know someone in this situation who was afraid that because of her damaged reputation, no priest would hear her confession. This is a long story that I will not tell you now. The worst of it was that these troubles did not just blow over. One person warned another not to have anything to do with her, so the trouble lasted the rest of her life. Some people did speak out in her favor, but they were few compared to the many who hated her!

But souls in the sixth Mansion actually receive more pain from praise than they do from false criticism. These souls know that any good they possess is a gift from God, since a short time ago they were weak in virtue and involved in terrible sin.

Suffering from Praise

Receiving praise can cause suffering, at least at first. Later, for reasons I will explain, the soul becomes almost as indifferent to praise as it is to accusations.

The first reason you become indifferent to praise is that personal experience proves men are as ready to speak well of you as they are to speak ill of you. As a result, you begin to attach no importance to one or the other.

Second, the soul in the sixth Mansion is enlightened by our Lord to understand that any good within it is a gift from God. So, when it is praised, the soul is oblivious to its role, praising God instead for the good work as if it had been done by another person.

The third reason the soul becomes indifferent to praise is because it understands God can use the praise to help others see their potential. When others understand our good work comes only from God, they believe it is possible that God could do the same in their lives.

Finally, because of what they have seen happen to others, beginners are often afraid that human praise may go to their heads. But with practice putting God's honor and glory first, they are cured of this temptation. And as a result, they also are cured of the pain that comes from false criticism and are content as long as God receives some praise in the end.

These and other reasons reduce the distress that comes from human praise. But human praise will always cause some discomfort until the soul becomes completely oblivious to the words of others. Most painful of all however, is undeserved praise.

When at last we become indifferent to praise, we become indifferent to false criticism. Criticism even becomes music to our ears. This is the amazing truth about our souls: They are strengthened, not intimidated, by blame and criticism. Personal experience helps us understand and appreciate the great gains that come from this path.

The soul learns that false criticism against it does not offend God, but God permits it for the benefit of the soul. The soul believes this so strongly that it even becomes affectionate toward those who falsely accuse them, considering them to be truer friends and greater helpers than those who speak well of them.

Physical Suffering

In this Mansion, our Lord may also send physical pain. If it is severe, this is the hardest of earthly trials, or at least exterior earthly trials. And severe physical pain can affect our spirit, too. The soul is in so much anguish it does not know what to do and would prefer to die by some quick martyrdom than continue to suffer. But God knows how much we can endure. He prepares us with patience and never sends us more pain than we can bear.

I know someone who, in addition to other trials, felt physical pain every day for forty years. True, she had led a sinful life, and these troubles felt small compared with the hell she knew she deserved. Those who have been less sinful may be led a different way, but I would always choose the way of suffering, if only to imitate our Lord Jesus Christ. In reality, we also receive many gains from suffering.

Interior Suffering

But physical suffering is minor compared to indescribable interior suffering. Let us first talk about the trial of meeting with a timid and inexperienced spiritual advisor. He is sure of nothing and fears everything. If he detects any imperfection in you, he suspects it is more than common sin. He thinks that in order to receive favor from God you must be an angel – which is impossible while we are in our bodies. And if you confess a sin, he blames the sin on the devil or our sad disposition. As to the latter, I am not surprised since there is so much despair in this world. The evil one often uses this to work harm, and spiritual advisors have good reason to be concerned and watchful.

But the poor soul is afraid of judgment. So, when it goes to its spiritual advisor as judge and is met with condemnation, it feels deep pain. Only someone with experience can understand this. For one of the most difficult trials – especially if the soul has lived a sinful life – is believing that God will allow them to be deceived into thinking they are forgiven, when in fact they are not. When they receive the grace of forgiveness, they only feel temporarily secure. They know forgiveness comes from the Spirit of God, but the memory of their sin haunts them. So, when they discover faults in themselves, this torturing regret returns.

This frequent suffering could be quieted by the reassurance of a wise spiritual advisor. But when their spiritual advisor only adds to their guilt, the pain is almost unbearable. Especially in this situation, spiritual dryness results. The soul feels as if it had never known God and will never know Him. When others talk about God, they seem to be talking about someone far away.

More pain is inflicted as the soul wonders if it deceived their advisor by not explaining its situation correctly. Even if it examines its conscience and believe it shared everything, it is of no use. Now that understanding has been dimmed, truth cannot be found. Imagination takes over.

And when imagination becomes master, the devil's lies seem true. The devil suggests God is allowing temptation and perhaps even rejecting them. This soul is in such intolerable anguish that I can compare it to nothing except perhaps the feeling of those lost in hell. For there is no comfort to be found in this storm.

If the soul goes to their spiritual advisor for comfort, it is as if all the demons assist him to torment it more. The spiritual advisor thinks, given the dangerous condition, he should be told whenever it suffers. But this only makes matters worse. The soul becomes incapable of acting on its own and loses all control. It is as if it knew how to read, but now it does not even know the alphabet. Eventually, the spiritual advisor realizes he does not know how to help.

There is no remedy to this trial except to wait for the mercy of God, who unexpectedly intervenes with a casual word or unforeseen circumstance. Immediately the cloud of trouble disappears, and the mind is full of light and happiness.

The soul praises God like one who emerges victorious from a dangerous battle. But it was He who won the victory, and the soul knows this. All the soul's weapons had been captured by the enemy. It realizes that if God ever abandons it, it would be completely powerless.

Better than any practice of meditation, this experience teaches this soul its utter weakness. The soul realizes the nothingness of human nature and what a miserable creature it is.

Grace may be hidden, but the truth is, this soul never fell from His grace. It did nothing to offend God. And it never wanted to offend God, even for earthly gain.

But so hidden is this grace that the sufferer believes that they have never loved God, and they never will. Any good they have done, or any past favor received from His Majesty, seems to be a dream or an imagination, while their sin stands clearly before them.

Oh, Jesus! How sad it is to see such a forsaken soul, and how few earthly comforts are available! Do not think, sisters, if you are ever in this condition, that rich and independent people have better remedies for this type of suffering. Absolutely not. It would be like reminding a condemned man with no time to live that he possesses all the joys of the world. Wealth increases this suffering.

Comfort can only come from above – nothing earthly can

help. God wants us to know our misery and that He is King. And this is important knowledge to prepare us for what lies ahead in the Castle.

What can the poor soul do if this trial does not go away? Prayer can't comfort a heart that is closed to receiving consolation. The mind can't understand the meaning of words prayed out loud. Mental prayer is out of the question because the faculties are incapable. And while solitude harms this soul, being with others creates fresh torment because as much as the suffering soul wants to hide its condition, it is weary and out of sorts.

How can the soul explain its indescribable suffering and spiritual affliction? The best remedy for these trials – and I do not mean deliverance from them, for our efforts will not deliver us – is to enable oneself to bear these trials by performing works of charity and trusting in the mercy of God. God will never fail those who hope in Him. May He be blessed forever! Amen.

Other Suffering

In this Mansion, the devil may bring other exterior trials which we will not mention since they are less common. For the most part they are less painful than other sufferings discussed because in these cases demons never paralyze the faculties or greatly disturb the soul. Because we understand demons can't harm the soul more than the Lord allows, this strength of reason prevents suffering caused by the deception of evil spirits. As long as the mind is in control, all suffering can be comparatively insignificant.

Later, when I explain different prayers and favors from our Lord in this Mansion, I will explain other types of suffering. Because of the effect on our body, some of these favors cause severe suffering. But they do not deserve to be called trials. Indeed, they are graces from God. In this Mansion the soul comes to recognize suffering as an undeserved favor and understands that it comes so that the soul may enter the final Mansion.

But it would be impossible to explain all the types of suffering in this Mansion. Nor could I ever explain them because they are of a different, higher level. And if I already have difficulty explaining the sufferings of a lower kind, how much less will I be able to explain the others. May God help me in all things, through the merits of His Son! Amen.

Two

Awakening our Soul to Love

It seems we deserted the little dove, but this is not the case. Suffering causes her to take higher flight. But before our Spouse unites her entirely to Himself, He increases her longing for Him so delicately that the soul does not realize what is happening.

This may be difficult to understand unless you have experienced it yourself, but these desires for God emerge as delicate and subtle impulses coming from the deepest part of the soul. I can't think of anything to compare them with. These favors are unlike anything we could obtain on our own and are completely different than the spiritual delights described in previous Mansions.

These graces awaken us to Him even when the mind is distracted and not thinking about God. His action is as quick as a falling comet. Like a thunderclap, even though no sound is heard, the soul knows it is being called by God. It understands this so well that especially at first, the soul trembles and may even cry out, even though there is no pain. It is conscious of receiving a delightful wound. It does not know how the wound arrived or who sent it, but it recognizes the wound is precious. The soul hopes the hurt will never heal and complains with words of love.

While this awakening makes us realize He is present, He does not reveal Himself so He may be enjoyed. This awakening is sweet and delightful, and the soul can't escape it even if it wished to. But it would never desire to escape. This favor is more delightful than the painless overpowering of the faculties during the prayer of quiet.

I am struggling, sisters, to help you understand this action of love. I do not even know how to explain it. For it seems like a contradiction to say that the Beloved would give the soul a clear understanding that He is close and unmistakably summoning us, yet He is beyond our reach in the seventh Mansion. When He speaks to us this way (which is not in words), activity in other Mansions stops, and the senses, imagination, and faculties do not dare move.

Oh, Almighty God! How profound are Your secrets and how unique spiritual things are from anything that can be seen or heard in this world! I can't find anything to compare with these graces, even though they may be insignificant compared to other graces You work in our souls.

This awakening of our soul so overwhelms the spirit that it dissolves in desire. Yet although it knows God is with it, it does not know what to ask. So, if this is the case, what more does the soul desire and why it is pained? What greater favor could it want? I do not know. I just know that the pain pierces the heart, and when He who wounded it draws out the dart, our love is so deep He seems to draw out the heart, too.

I have been thinking that God is like a burning furnace who sends a small spark into the soul. The soul feels the heat of this great fire, but the heat is not enough to consume it. The spirit lingers in the delightful burn of the spark. This seems to me to be the best comparison I can find for this awakening, for the pain is not really pain at all. Sometimes it lasts a long time, and other times it passes quickly. This is as God chooses because it can't be controlled with human effort.

The little spark never wholly inflames the spirit, but when the soul is ready to take fire, the spark suddenly dies out, leaving the heart longing to suffer again in pangs of love. This favor does not have a natural origin and is not caused by our emotions. It also is not imagined or an illusion from the devil. Its effects do not resemble those that come from other devotions in which our joy makes us question reality. Undoubtedly, this awakening of our heart arises from the place in our soul where our unchangeable God dwells.

When you experience this favor, your senses and faculties are not suspended. You wonder at what is happening and do nothing to prevent it. But I do not think you could do anything to prevent or increase this delightful pain. Anyone who has received this favor from our Lord knows what I am talking about. Sincerely thank Him. Do not be afraid that you imagined this favor but be afraid of not being grateful.

And then strive to better your entire life and serve Him, and you will see the results and many more blessings. I know a person who passed several years only experiencing this favor, and she was perfectly satisfied. Even if she had been suffering severe trials, she would have felt abundantly repaid. May He be forever blessed! Amen!

You may wonder why, compared to other favors, we can feel more certain that this favor is not a deception by the devil. I think there are several reasons.

First, the devil can't cause us to feel suffering and joy simultaneously. He may cause what appears to be spiritual pleasure, but he can't join suffering – and sometimes intense suffering – to the peace and joy of the soul. His power is only external. The pain the devil causes is accompanied by anxiety and struggle.

Second, this welcome suffering comes in a Mansion in which Satan has no power.

Third, the devil would not deceive us with an experience that produces great benefits for our souls – mainly, the resolution and longing to suffer for God. As a result of these favors, the soul is far more determined to put aside earthly pleasures and distractions.

In addition to the certainty that this favor is not a deception of the devil, it is also very clear to the soul that this favor is not fiction. The imagination may try to counterfeit some favors, but not this one. The experience is too real for there to be any doubt. If you are uncertain, then you can be sure you did not receive this favor because the awakening is felt as clearly as a loud voice in your ears. It is impossible for these experiences to come from emotions because emotions only create imagination. This favor comes from the interior of the soul.

I may be mistaken on this, but I will not change my opinion unless I hear something to the contrary from someone who understands these matters. I know someone who was very fearful about being deceived but was never concerned about deception in this state of prayer.

Our Lord may rouse our souls in other ways. For example, a person may be praying out loud and not thinking about themselves when they are suddenly seized by a delightful feeling as if they were overcome with a fragrance that permeates all the senses. I do not mean there really is a fragrance, but this resembles how the Spouse makes His presence known. It moves the soul to the desire of enjoying Him, thus preparing it for difficult acts of love and sincere praise of our Lord.

This favor comes from the same source as the previous one mentioned, but the soul experiences nothing about it that causes pain, including the desire to enjoy Him. And for reasons already given, nothing causes fear, but one should receive this favor with gratitude.

Three

Other Ways of Awakening the Soul

God has other ways of awakening the soul. Although they may seem to be a greater favor, they can be dangerous, so I will explain them in detail.

God may awaken us through words heard by the soul in several different ways. The words may seem to come from the inner depths of the soul or from the superior part of the soul. Or words may appear to come from outside oneself, and even heard like a real voice.

Most of the time these voices are only imagined – especially by people who are emotional or imaginative. I think we should not pay attention to some people when they say they see, hear, or learn things supernaturally. But do not upset them by saying that what they report comes from the devil. Instead, listen as though they are sick people. Spiritual people should tell them these visions are unnecessary for the service of God and to pay no attention. They should be reminded that the devil has deceived many Christians this way, and while this might not be true in their case, they should not trouble themselves about it anymore.

But be careful not to aggravate an emotional person by telling them it was only their imagination. They will continue believing it was real because it seemed real to them. The solution is to encourage these types of people to moderate their time in prayer and persuade them to ignore their "visions." The devil may use these weak souls to injure others, even if they themselves escape unhurt.

Both weak and strong souls should be cautious about these communications until it is certain which spirit is behind them. I believe in the beginning it is better to resist them entirely. If they come from God, they will increase, otherwise they will just stop. At the same time, our souls should be open and at peace, recognizing these communications are beyond our control.

Distinguishing Communications from God

Words heard by the soul may come from God, the devil, or the imagination. With the help of God, I will try to describe how to distinguish among them, and when they are dangerous. It is important that we understand this since there are many prayerful souls who hear them.

But sisters, there is no harm in believing or disbelieving these voices if they are only for your benefit. If the words only console you or warn you about your faults, then it does not matter where they came from. One caution – although these words may come from God, you must not think more highly of yourself for receiving them. Remember, Christ spoke to the Pharisees too. Good comes from what you do with His words, not that He spoke them to you.

And do not pay attention to words you hear that contradict the Holy Scriptures. Reject those words as though they come from Satan himself. Even if the words only come from your imagination, treat them as if they were tempting your faith, and resist them. If you ignore them, they will stop.

Returning to the first point, discerning if the voices come from God does not depend on whether the voices come from outside oneself or from the inferior or superior part of the soul. In my opinion, there are instead three sure indications that these voices come from God.

The first and truest is that the words carry power and authority, for the voice of God leaves an effect. For example, a soul may find itself suffering sorrow and anxiety while the mind is dark and drained. But when it hears the words, "be not troubled," it is immediately filled with light. These words alone deliver the soul from all its pain, even if no one else, including theologians, could persuade it to be at peace.

Or take a person who is troubled and terrified by people who tell her she is under the influence of the devil. She hears, "It is I, be not afraid," and at once she loses all her fears. She believes no one could make her fearful again. Finally, a person anxious about the success of important business matters hears the words, "be at peace, all will go well," and they are immediately reassured and free from anxiety. Many other examples could be mentioned, but in all these examples, the power and authority of the voice of God is clear by its effect.

The second sign that these voices are from God is the great calm, devout and peaceful memory that lingers in the soul along with a desire to praise God. They say that communications in this Mansion are not uttered by God but come through an angel. My God, if Your word delivered by a messenger has such power, then what power You leave in the soul united with You in the mutual bond of love.

The third proof is that these words remain in the memory for a very long time, sometimes never to be forgotten. This is not the case with words from mere men. No matter how important and educated they may be, men's words are rarely impressed upon our memory.

If the voice heard predicts things to come and their fulfillment seems utterly impossible, the soul retains an unyielding certainty that they will be fulfilled. Everything may work against what was predicted and years may go by, but the soul never loses its belief that God will find the means to accomplish them. The soul believes that what was heard will come to pass, as it eventually does.

Still, as I said, the soul is troubled when it sees obstacles to fulfillment. The effect of the words and the assurance they leave convinces us at that moment that they came from God. Later we may have doubts, even if at first we would have died defending what we believe to be true. We wonder if the words came from the devil or from our imagination. These doubts must be suggestions from the evil one to trouble and intimidate us. This is especially true if the words would be difficult to carry out but regard a business matter that would bring blessing to many souls or works that would bring great honor and service to God. When will Satan relent? At the very least he weakens our faith, and it harms us to doubt that God has the power to work beyond our understanding.

Despite the devil's attacks, obstacles, and spiritual advisors who tell us it was just our imagination, we still have a flicker of certainty that the words we heard were true. I do not know where this faith comes from, but even if all other hope dies, nothing can put out this heartfelt spark of faith. When at last our Lord's words are accomplished, the soul is so satisfied and joyful that it can only praise His Majesty. And the praise does not come from seeing the actual event come to pass (even if it is important), but that His words have proved true.

I do not know why it is so important to the soul that His words prove true. I think some people believe that if the words do not come to pass, then it is like getting caught telling a lie. But all you did was repeat what was said to you. This reminds us of the prophet Jonah, who was upset when his prophesy of the destruction of Nineveh was prevented by God's mercy.[51]

In fact, since these words come from the Spirit of God, it is right to trust them. It is right to desire that He who is supreme truth is never seen as a deceiver. So, it is no wonder that the hearer of the words rejoices when the words are accomplished after a thousand delays and difficulties. Better to suffer to see the words fulfilled then to never see their fulfillment. Perhaps not everyone has this weakness, but I personally do not find fault with it.

However, if we only imagined the words, we receive no such signs of conviction, peace, or inner joy. I have come across people who think they hear or see things from God when they are in deep prayer and their senses are dormant and unconscious of anything external. Maybe they have a weak constitution or a vivid imagination, but what they remember has no more effect on them than an ordinary

---

[51] Jonah 4

dream. It often happens that someone who lovingly asks our Lord for something believes they hear what they want to hear.

A person accustomed to receiving divine communication can discern when it is only their imagination. But we also need to fear the possibility that the communication is coming from the devil. If the signs mentioned hold true, we can be fairly certain that the message came from God. But if the words or signs are telling us to do something significant, or if they concern another person, we should not act on them until we talk to a spiritual advisor who is both wise and a servant of God.

Even if we are certain the words are true and they were repeated to us several times, we should be cautious to obey. His Majesty wants us to be cautious – this is not disobedience to His commands. Even if we feel certain, He provides His representatives to help us take courageous action.[52] Our Lord will help our spiritual advisors know if the message is coming from His Spirit. If they think it is not, then we have no obligation to obedience. I believe it would be dangerous to ignore our spiritual advisor's opinion and prefer our own. So, sisters, I warn you not to do this.

Authenticating Intellectual Visions

Another way God may speak to the soul is through an *intellectual vision*, which I also believe comes from Him. I will describe it more later. This communication happens

---

[52] Luke 10:16

secretly in a deep place in the soul. Through spiritual hearing, clear words come from our Lord Himself. The way the soul understands these words and the effects they produce convince us that they could not have come from the devil. The powerful effect they have on us also convinces us that they did not come from our imagination.

The soul can be assured an intellectual vision comes from God for the following reasons.

First, the language is so clear that the soul remembers every syllable, how it was said, and every word used in a sentence. If it had only been our imagination, it would not be as audible or distinct, but only like something half-dreamed.

Second, while the message may have something to do with a previous thought, it comes unexpectedly when you were not thinking about it, such as in the middle of a conversation. Often it relates to something the hearer never knew or imagined could happen. It is impossible for the imagination to fabricate something it never thought about or desired.

Third, in a genuine intellectual vision, the soul hears the words, whereas something imagined comes gradually as you compose what you want to hear.

Fourth, the words are different because each one comes with immense meaning. Our intellect alone could never compose such depth of meaning so quickly.

Finally, in a manner I can't explain, these communications frequently give us far more understanding than words alone. I will talk more about this way of understanding later, for it is something very subtle for which we should thank God.

Some people are very suspicious of communications like

these. A certain person who experienced these communications was doubtful and did not understand them. Because she frequently received this favor, she was able to study them carefully.

In the beginning, her greatest doubt was that the vision came from her imagination. It was easier to know when they came from the devil even though he can imitate the spirit of light. The devil says words very clearly so there is no doubt to their meaning. But Satan can never create the effects I just mentioned or leave peace and light in the soul. Satan's words only create anxiety and confusion. And he can do little or no harm to a person who is humble enough to realize the vision might not be from God, and as I advised, does not act on what is heard.

If your soul receives words of favor and consolation, be careful how you respond. If you consider yourself special for this, then examine yourself carefully. Unless humility increases with God's expressions of love for you, then the words do not come from the Holy Spirit. In divine communication, typically the greater the favors, the humbler the soul feels as it keenly remembers its sins. The soul loses self-interest. The will and memory more intensely seek God's honor with no thought of self. The soul also becomes increasingly careful not to deliberately deviate from God's will, and more certain that it deserves condemnation rather than the favors of God.

When these effects follow, the soul should not be alarmed by the favors experienced during prayer. Rather, it should be confident in the mercy of God who is faithful and will not allow the devil's deception.[53] But it is always good to be on your guard.

Those who do not receive communications like this from our Lord may think that to avoid danger, the soul should stop listening or find distractions. This only works if the visions come from your imagination, in which case they can be prevented by not desiring or paying attention to them. But it is impossible to do this when the communications come from the Holy Spirit, whose voice stops our thoughts and forces our minds to listen.

I believe a person with good hearing can easily block out a loud voice by distracting themselves or thinking about something else. But it is impossible to do that when the Holy Spirit speaks. The soul is powerless to do anything but listen. For He who can stop the sun on its course at the prayer of Joshua can quiet us completely and make us aware of a stronger Lord who governs our Castle.[54] There is no remedy. The voice brings us to deep devotion and humility. May God provide a remedy that would help us forget ourselves and only aim to please Him. Amen.

God grant that I have succeeded in explaining what I hoped and that it may be some guide to those who experience these favors.

---

[53] 1 Corinthians 10:13
[54] Joshua 10:12-13

Four

With all the trials and other things mentioned, what rest can the poor little butterfly find? Our suffering increases our desire for the Bridegroom. His Majesty, aware of our weakness, strengthens the soul with these trials and many others in order to give it the courage to be joined with so great a Lord and take Him as its Spouse.

Perhaps you will laugh and think I am talking foolishly. It seems there is no need for courage. There is no woman so miserable who would not have the courage to marry a king. Perhaps this is true if he was an earthly king. But you need more courage than you think to unite with the King of heaven. Our nature is too timid and lowly for someone so great.

I am certain that unless God gives us courage, it would be impossible for us to receive the favor of our marriage to Him, even if we understood all the benefits.

Raptures

I will explain how His Majesty concludes our marriage in this Mansion, which I understand happens through raptures that engulf the soul so that one's senses and faculties are overcome. If the senses and faculties are not overcome, I think being close to so mighty a Sovereign could kill us.

I am speaking of genuine raptures, not the imagination of weak people which occurs so often these days. As I have said, some people are so emotional that the prayer of quiet is enough to overwhelm them.

I would like to describe several types of raptures which I learned from discussions with many spiritual people. I do not know if I will succeed in explaining them as I did when I wrote about them elsewhere. But it seems worthwhile to repeat what I have said about raptures and other things that happen in this Mansion, if for no other reason than to keep this information in the proper order.

In one type of rapture of the soul, a person (who may not be in prayer at the time), is struck by some word they remember or hear about God. His Majesty is moved by the person's long-suffering desire for Him. Somehow God increases the spark I described in the interior of the spirit until it entirely inflames the soul. The soul rises with new life like a phoenix from the flames and humbly believes all its sins are forgiven. The purified soul is united with God in a way only known to Him and the soul, although the soul would not be able to explain it afterward.

The mind, while overwhelmed, does not lose control. A rapture is not like fainting where nothing is felt on the inside or outside. What I know is that the soul in rapture is never more alive to spiritual things or so full of light and knowledge of His Majesty. This seems impossible – if the faculties and senses are so absorbed, how does the soul understand this mystery? I do not know, and perhaps only the Creator knows.

There are many mysteries in these last two Mansions. And there actually is no closed door between this Mansion and the last. The door between them is wide open. However, since some things in the last rooms are only shown to those who travel far enough, I thought it would be better to divide them.

Imaginative and Intellectual Visions

While the soul is in suspension during a rapture, our Lord favors it by revealing heavenly mysteries and *imaginative visions* – visions we receive in the form of images seen by the eyes of our soul. These secrets can be described afterward because they are so imprinted on the memory that they are not forgotten.

But when the vision received during rapture is an *intellectual vision*, it is much more difficult to share. These visions may so sublime it might not be possible for someone on earth to describe them. However, since the soul still has possession over its senses, it can say many things about these intellectual visions.

You may not know what visions are, especially an intellectual one. I will explain them later in this Mansion since I have been asked to do so by someone with authority. The explanation may seem unnecessary, but it might be useful to some people.

You will ask me, "If an intellectual vision given by our Lord in this Mansion can't be described, what good are they?" Oh, daughters! Their value cannot be understated. For even though the recipient will struggle to describe them, they are imprinted in the soul and never forgotten. But you may ask, "How can they be remembered if no image is seen and our faculties do not understand them?" I do not understand this either, but I know that even if the recipient did not believe in God or only felt obliged to believe in Him, after this experience the soul would worship Him.

During an intellectual vision, the truths about the greatness of God are impressed upon the soul and cause it to worship Him. This is what happened when the patriarch Jacob worshipped God after he was shown the ladder.[55] The ladder must have revealed many other secrets he did not know how to explain. Jacob could not have discovered these secrets just by watching angels ascending and descending a ladder.

Nor was Moses able to explain all he saw in the burning bush, but only what God wished him to describe.[56] But the soul of Moses must have seen other mysteries, including the certainty that God was present in the burning bush. The lawgiver could never have undertaken so many great trials without this understanding. Wonderful revelations of God in the thorns of the bush gave Moses the courage for his great deeds on behalf of the children of Israel.

Sisters, we do not have to find reasons to understand the secrets of God. If we believe Him to be Almighty, then be convinced that we can't comprehend His wonders – especially since we are worms with limited intelligence. Let us praise Him for allowing us to understand some of them.

I wish I could find an example to help you understand these intellectual visions during rapture. None seems appropriate, but I will try the following. Imagine entering a treasure chamber belonging to a king or great nobleman. In it are a vast number of objects of glass, porcelain, and other precious things, arranged so you see them all at once when you enter the room.

---

[55] Genesis 28:12
[56] Exodus 3:1-16

I entered a room like this while I was visiting the house of the Duchess of Alba (where obedience required me to stay because she insisted to my superiors). I stood amazed when I entered. I wondered what use there could be of so many trinkets, but then I realized the sight of so many different objects should cause me to praise God. I laugh to myself now realizing that seeing them provides a useful example.

Although I was in the room for a long time, there were so many objects that while I remember the sight of the whole collection, I could not now describe a single object or what it was made of. Something like this happens when the soul is closely united to God in an intellectual vision.

The soul is placed in this heavenly room in the Mansion – which must be at the center of our soul where God resides. Clearly the soul has some of these rooms since God dwells within it. It is enough that the soul is full of joy in the encounter, so the Lord withholds other secrets in this moment. But sometimes, He is pleased to pull back some of the joy so the soul can absorb other things in the room. When the mind returns to itself, it can recall what it saw, but the details are indescribable. It can't see any more of the supernatural than what God chose to reveal.

So, am I saying that the soul is seeing an imaginative vision – a vision given in images? Absolutely not. I am talking about an intellectual vision. I am so ignorant and slow, perhaps I can't explain anything well. But I know if I say it clearly it could not come from me.

Effects of Genuine Raptures

I think if the soul does not learn a mystery at any time during a rapture, then it is not a true rapture but a result of a natural weakness. This may occur in people with delicate health or those who go into a stupor during the prayer of quiet, as I have said, because any act of the spirit overpowers their weak physical nature.

This is not true of genuine raptures. In this case God carries off the soul for Himself. As the soul is now His very own bride, He shows her some small part of the kingdom that she has won through their union. No matter how little it is, everything about this great God is magnificent.

He will not allow the power of the senses to become an obstacle to this moment. The doors of all the Mansions are closed at once, leaving open only the room He is in so we may enter. Blessed is such mercy. Those who do not desire this favor and who have lost our Lord are rightfully cursed.

Oh, my sisters! We have nothing worth doing or holding on to compared to our God who desires to reveal Himself to a worm! And if we hope to enjoy this blessing during our lifetimes, what are we doing? Why do we delay? What would stop us, even for a moment, in searching for our Lord, like the bride who looked through the streets and squares for her Bridegroom?[57]

Everything in this world that does not lead us to this Mansion is foolishness! Even if all earthly pleasures, riches, and happiness could last for eternity, they would be

---

[57] Song of Solomon 3:1-2

disappointing compared to these treasures which will be enjoyed forever. And they are nothing compared with possessing the Lord of treasures in heaven and earth.

Oh, our human blindness! When will this dust be removed from our eyes? Although we think the dust does not blind us, some specks are left behind and spread, causing us great harm. For the love of God, my sisters, let our faults convince us of our misery. Let those faults be like the clay our Spouse used to open the eyes of the blind man.[58] Realizing our imperfections, let us beg Him to bring good from our weakness so we can please Him in all things.

Forgive me, sisters, as I have wandered unconsciously from my subject. Believe me, when I speak of these wonders of God's greatness, I can't help but feel saddened at what we lose by our own fault. It is true that His Majesty grants these favors to those He chooses. But if we sought Him like He seeks us, He would give all these favors to us. He longs to give His blessings to souls. Sharing His gifts cannot diminish His riches.

Let us return to what happens during a rapture in this Mansion. By the command of the Bridegroom, the doors of the Mansion, and even those of the keep and the whole Castle, are closed. When He decides to carry off the soul, He takes away the breath. Other senses may last longer, but no words can be uttered.

Occasionally, the senses are lost immediately. As if the soul has left the body, the hands and body become cold, and no

---

[58] John 9:6-7

breathing is detected. This deep suspension only lasts a short while and the body gradually comes back to itself. It returns from this death with more vigorous life in the soul.

Even though this blessing ends quickly, it leaves the will so intoxicated that the mind is transported out of itself for a day or several days. Such a person finds they are only capable of acting with love for God. Even though they are wide awake, they seem asleep to earthly concerns. And when the soul completely returns to itself, it is astonished to have received such a gift, and it desires to serve God in any way He asks!

Since favors in earlier Mansions left effects on the soul, what are the effects of this greater favor? The soul wishes it had a thousand lives to live for God, and that every tongue on earth would join in praising Him. It longs for great trials no matter their severity, for the power of love prevents them from being felt. The soul realizes that martyrs did not suffer, since with the Lord's help, pain is easy. So, the soul complains to His Majesty if it is not suffering.

When God sends this rapture in secret, we consider it a favor. If it is witnessed by others, however, shame and confusion can diminish the blessing. Witnesses may judge that the rapture did not come from God, and so God does not receive the praise due to Him. Although this shame and confusion are unavoidable, I believe it shows a lack of personal humility. If we truly want to be humble, why should we care what others think?

Our Lord once told someone who was troubled by these thoughts, "Do not be disturbed. People will either praise Me or condemn you. In either case, you benefit." She was greatly encouraged and comforted by these words, and I share them in case they help others suffering in the same way.

Apparently, our Lord wants all people to know that this soul is His own, and no one can hurt it. People are welcome to attack the person's body, honor, and possessions, for God receives glory if they do. But the soul itself can't be attacked unless it withdraws from the protection of the Spouse. God will defend the soul against the whole world and hell besides.

I do not know if I have succeeded in explaining raptures. As I said, explaining a genuine rapture is impossible, but I think nothing was lost in trying. The effects left by "false" raptures are very different. I do not call them false because people who experience them want to deceive others, but because they themselves are unknowingly deceived. The signs and effects of a false rapture do not produce the effects of the true blessing. But raptures have become so discredited that when the Lord does bestow the favor, no one believes it anyway. May He be forever blessed and praised. Amen, amen!

Five

Flight of the Spirit

There is another form of rapture which, although it is essentially the same as the last, produces a different feeling in the soul. I call it the *flight of the spirit* because the soul suddenly feels a rapid sense of motion. The spirit seems to be hurrying away at an alarming speed, especially at first. The soul experiencing this favor must have courage, as well as faith, trust, and resignation to God's purpose.

You can imagine the dismay of a soul in perfect possession of its senses that suddenly finds itself rising, and even sometimes its body, too. It does not know where the spirit is going, who is raising it, or how it is happening. In the first moments, the soul is not certain if it is from God. Can it be resisted? No, I have been told any resistance only accelerates the motion.

The soul that receives the flight of the spirit has often, earnestly, and willingly placed itself in His hands. Now God appears to be teaching this soul that it no longer belongs to itself. If there is any opposition to the flight, the soul is snatched away more quickly. A person who tried to resist resolved to yield herself in the hands of the Almighty if it happened again. We should have as little resistance as metal drawn to a magnet.

In the flight of the spirit, it is as though there is a sudden change in the bowl of water from the fourth Mansion that had been gently and quietly filled. Now our great God, who restrains the rivers and holds oceans in their boundaries, lets loose the streams.[59] In a powerful rush, the waters flow into the bowl, and a mighty wave rises with enough power to lift the vessel of our soul. Neither the ship, pilot, nor sailors can control the fury of the sea. As a powerless ship on these waters can't be stopped, the interior part of the soul can't stop. The senses or faculties can only do what is commanded by Him Who holds them.

Sisters, just by writing this I am amazed by the power on display by this great King and Emperor. Think about the feelings of those who have this experience! I am convinced that if His Majesty revealed Himself to the greatest sinners this way, they would never dare offend Him again – if not because of love, then because of fear.

Those who are taught in such a wonderful manner are bound to work hard not to displease such a Master! In His name, I beg you sisters not to be content with just receiving this experience. Remember, someone who has been given much owes much.[60]

Courage in Self-Knowledge

Great courage is needed because this favor is frightening. This thought should also terrify our souls: Unless we receive courage from our Lord, we suffer great and constant grief remembering everything His Majesty has done for us and how

---

[59] Proverbs 8:29
[60] Luke 12:48

little good we have done. Anything we accomplish is pathetic since it is full of fault, failure, and weakness.

To block the memory of our imperfect good deeds (if we, indeed, have any), we wish to forget about them altogether. Instead, we only want to think about our sin and cast ourselves on the mercy of God. We can't repay our debt to Him, and we beg for the pity and compassion He always shows to sinners.

Maybe He will respond as He did to someone thinking about this while kneeling before a crucifix. She never felt she had anything to offer or sacrifice for Him. The Crucified One consoled her by saying He had given her all the sufferings and trials of His Passion so she could have them as her own to offer to His Father. She was comforted and enriched by these words, which she will never forget. Whenever she thinks about her sinfulness, she is encouraged and consoled by remembering these words.

I could give examples of other experiences like this from many holy and prayerful persons I have known, but I will not share them in case you think they relate to me. This example is instructive because it shows how we can please our Lord through our self-knowledge. Self-knowledge reminds us of our poverty and sinfulness. It reminds us that all we have comes from Him.

Therefore, sisters, courage is needed to receive this self-knowledge and the spiritual favors that come to a soul brought by our Lord to these final Mansions. I think the soul who is humble requires great courage to face the knowledge of one's misery. May God give us this humility for His Name's sake.

Effects of the Flight of the Spirit

Let us return to the sudden flight of the spirit. The soul appears to have left the body, although the body is not lifeless. Yet for a few moments it can't tell if its spirit remains with the body. The soul feels transported to another place where the wonders and light are so unique that they could not be imagined. In an instant, its mind learns many things all at once. Even if the imagination and intellect spent years trying to list them all, the soul would only remember a small fraction of what it saw.

This is not an intellectual vision, but an imaginative vision. Images are seen through the eyes of the soul more clearly than earthly things are seen by our bodily eyes. Although no words are said, the spirit learns many truths. For example, if it sees any saints, it knows them as well as if they had spoken often.

Other times during the flight of the spirit, it sees things beyond what the eyes of the soul perceive through an intellectual vision. Neither the bodily eyes nor the eyes of the soul see anything, but by some wonderful intuition I can't explain, we see our Lord accompanied by a host of angels. Maybe those who have experienced this favor can explain it better.

During the flight of the spirit, I can't tell if the soul stays in the body or not. I have often thought that the soul and spirit (which are one) are like the sun that stays in the heavens as its rays reach the earth.[61] Thus, while the soul remains in place, the higher part of the soul is raised up. I do not understand what I am explaining, but the truth is, the interior of the soul travels upward as fast as a bullet from a gun. I do not know another word to use but "flight."

Although noiseless, the flight is so clearly a movement of the soul that it can't be the work of the imagination. And while the spirit is far outside of itself, great mysteries are revealed. When the senses return, the benefits it feels are remarkable. It is convinced that the world holds nothing of value compared to what it has seen. From this point forward, life is painful, and earthly things that seemed important are now uncared for and unnoticed.

The first children of Israel who were sent into the promised land returned with souvenirs.[62] In the same way, during these experiences our Lord seems to show the soul something about the land to which it is traveling. Now that the soul knows where it will rest, it has courage to pass through the painful trials of the journey. You may think this benefit can't be gained so quickly, but those who have had this experience understand that this is what happens.

The clear proofs that this is not the work of the devil or the imagination are the peace, calm and good fruits left in the soul, as well as three other graces.

First, what we see during the flight of the spirit helps us understand more of God's greatness.

---

[61] 2 Corinthians 12:2-4
[62] Numbers 13:18-27

Second, we gain self-knowledge and humility by seeing how creatures as low as we compare with the Creator of such wonders. How dare we offend Him or even think about looking up at Him?

The third grace is the increase in our disregard for any earthly thing not dedicated to the service of our great God.

With such jewels the Bridegroom decorates His bride. They are too valuable for her to keep them carelessly. These visions are so deeply engraved that I believe she can never forget them. Losing them would be a tragedy. But the Spouse Who gave her these gifts has the power to provide the grace not to lose them.

I told you courage was required by the soul. Do you think it is a small thing for the spirit to feel separated from the body, not knowing why it is losing its senses? It is necessary that He who gives all things should also give us courage. You will say this fear is rewarded, and I agree.

May He who gives such favors be forever praised, and may His Majesty give us the courage to be worthy of serving Him. Amen.

Six

Longing for God

As a result of all these splendid favors, the soul in this Mansion longs to fully enjoy Him who gives these favors. Life becomes a painful, although wonderful, torture. Death would be welcomed gladly when everything about this exile on earth seems difficult. With tears, the soul begs God to remove it from the world. Solitude becomes a temporary comfort, but grief soon returns as a companion whose temporary absences feel strange.

This poor little butterfly can't find a lasting place of rest. So tender is her love for God that at the slightest provocation it catches fire, and the soul takes flight. In this Mansion, raptures are common. And they can't be prevented in public, so gossip and persecution follow.

Despite effort, this soul still is not free of fear. Unfortunately, there are many people who feed these fears, especially other spiritual people. On one hand, she has great confidence in her soul, especially when she is alone with God. But on the other hand, she wonders if she is being deceived by the devil and offending Him who she loves deeply. She does not mind her spiritual advisors' criticisms of her experiences. She does what they tell her to do and asks everyone to pray for her. And she begs His Majesty to lead her on a path that is not so dangerous.

But no matter the danger, the benefits of these favors are

so great that she knows they lead her on the path to heaven. Everything she has read, heard, or learned about God's law confirms this. So, no matter how she tries, she can't stop desiring the favors from God experienced in this Mansion. She is sorry that this is against her spiritual advisor's counsel because she believes disobedience leads to deception. While she would rather be cut into pieces than willfully sin, she suffers believing her desire for these spiritual favors may unknowingly cause her to repeatedly sin.

God gives these souls an intense desire to please Him in even the smallest matter. To escape sin, they try to avoid society when possible, and envy people who live in the wilderness. On the other hand, they hope that if they live among others, they can help even one soul praise God more. Women are frustrated by the barriers of gender and envy men allowed to teach everyone about the mighty God of hosts.

The poor little butterfly has so many chains it can't fly away! God have pity on her. Guide her path so she may be able to accomplish some of her desires for Your honor and glory! Ignore how little she deserves and her sinful nature. You have the power, Lord, to make the great sea and the wide Jordan River roll back for the children of Israel.[63] Yet do not spare her suffering, because supported by Your strength she can endure many trials. And she has the resolution and desire to endure them.

Stretch forth Your arm, oh Lord, to help her so her life

---

[63] Exodus 14:21-22, Joshua 3:13-17

won't be wasted on insignificant things.[64] Let Your greatness appear in this weak woman, so men, seeing that she is sinful, will praise You for it! And let it cost her a lot – as much as she wishes – for she longs to lose a thousand lives to lead one soul to praise you more. A life lost for this purpose would be well spent. She knows the truth – she is unworthy to bear even the lightest cross, and less worthy to die for You.

Sisters, I never intended to share this, and do not know why I have or what made me. You must know that thoughts like this are bound to come from the deeper spiritual experiences in this Mansion. These experiences produce permanent, not temporary, desire for God. This desire proves genuine when opportunities arise and are acted upon.

But how can I say that our desire for God is permanent, when sometimes the soul is afraid of even small things and is too frightened to undertake any work for God? I believe our Lord is doing good by leaving the soul to its natural weakness. The soul in this state recognizes that any strength it has comes from His Majesty. This clear truth destroys all pride as the Lord reveals to us sinners a deeper understanding of His mercy and greatness. But usually, our soul stays in a condition of fear.

Dangers in our Longing for God

Beware, sisters, as this great longing to be with our Lord is sometimes so distressful it consumes us. This desire should be controlled rather than encouraged. However, this can be

[64] Genesis 8:8-9

impossible, as I will talk about later.

In this Mansion control over our longing for God is still possible because of our desire to conform to the will of God. Remember what Saint Martin said: "Oh, Lord, if I am still necessary to Your people, I do not want to escape my life; Your will be done." If your longing for God becomes oppressive, remember his words and control your thoughts.

This anguished longing for God seems to be found in people who are spiritually advanced. Perhaps the devil excites our desire for God just to fool us into thinking we are spiritually advanced. In any case, it is wise to be cautious.

I personally do not think the devil brings the feeling of peace and joy that accompanies this longing for God. Instead, the false longing he gives comes with discontent, as happens when we suffer over worldly things. A person who has known both feelings will understand the difference. But someone who is less advanced might think that a deep, suffering longing for God is a good thing, when in fact it can become unhealthy if this longing is continual.

You should consider that these longings in our soul also may be caused by emotional weakness, especially among sensitive people who cry over every small trouble. These people constantly imagine they are crying for God's sake when they are doing no such thing. Sometimes any mention or thought of God results in fits of uncontrollable weeping. The cause may be their emotional weakness, which is more likely the source of their tears than their love of God. They never seem to stop crying, and since they believe their tears are somehow helpful, they do not try to get them under control or to distract themselves. The devil grasps this opportunity to weaken them so that they are unable to pray and maintain spiritual disciplines.

I think you must be puzzled by what I am saying. You may wonder what you should do since I see danger in everything. If I see danger in something as good as tears, perhaps I am the one who has been deceived! But I say this only because I have witnessed these false tears in others, although not myself. In my own case, there is nothing tender about me, and my heart is so hard that it often grieves me. However, when the fire burns fiercely within, stony as my heart may be, it breaks easily. Tears from this source are soothing and gentle and rarely do harm. As long as there is humility, the only harm done by false tears is to the body, not the soul. When humility is missing, it is good to be on guard for danger.

We should not think that if we cry a lot we have done all we need to do. Rather, we must work hard and cultivate virtue. This is all that matters. Allow tears to fall when God sends them, without forcing yourself to shed them. Then, if we do not pay much attention to them, the tears will leave the parched soil of our soul fertile for good fruit, for this is the water which falls from heaven. No matter how we dig, we will never find water like this. We may work and search until we are exhausted without finding a puddle, much less an abundant well!

Therefore, sisters, I believe it is best to put ourselves in the presence of God, consider His mercy and grandeur and our own sinfulness, and leave Him to give us what He wills. He knows best what is good for us, whether it is water or drought.

With this attitude we can enjoy peace, and the devil has less opportunity to deceive us.

Jubilation of the Soul

In the midst of these experiences that are both painful and delightful at the same time, our Lord sometimes causes a mysterious jubilation in our soul and a strange type of prayer it does not understand. If He gives you this grace, praise Him! I am describing it for you so you will know that it is something real.

I believe in these moments of jubilation the faculties of our soul closely unite to God, and He leaves both the faculties and the senses free to rejoice. When this happens, they do not understand how or what they are enjoying.

This may sound like nonsense, but it really happens. The soul has so much joy that it will not enjoy it alone. The joy spills over to the senses, and it wants to share it with others so they will join in praising God, too.

What praise and demonstrations of joy come from this person just so others might know that happiness! They wish, like the father of the prodigal son, to invite all their friends to celebrate that their soul is in its rightful place.[65] For at least at this moment, the soul's security seems certain. And I believe this is true. The devil can't bring such joy and peace to the center of our being. Our entire delight is in urging others to praise God.

It would require painful effort to silence this impulsive joy.

---

[65] Luke 15:22-32

Saint Francis must have had this experience when despite an attack by robbers, he ran through the fields crying out that he was the "herald of the great King." Perhaps other saints went to the desert so that, like Saint Francis, they could freely proclaim God's praise.

I knew Fray Peter of Alcántara used to have these jubilation experiences. Because of the life he led, I believe he was a saint, but people often though he was crazy when they heard him. Oh, what happy madness, sisters! If only God would give it to all of us!

And what a favor He has shown you in placing you in this house of sisters. If you receive this jubilation blessing and you tell others, no one will think you are crazy. If you were living in the world where men rarely hear God praised, it would be scandalous.

We have such a miserable life in this world! How blessed are those who are momentarily freed from it. It delights me when I see you together praising God and feeling great joy for being in this convent. It is clear your praises come from the depths of your souls. I would like you to do this often, sisters, for when one begins, it causes the rest to imitate. There is no better way for our tongues to be used than praising God who has given us so many reasons to praise Him.

May His Majesty often give us this type of prayer. It is safe and beneficial. But we can't acquire it on our own, as it is something supernatural. Sometimes the jubilation can last for the entire day. The soul goes about like someone drunk, although the senses are still sharp. It is like what happens when we are depressed, and our imagination can't stop dwelling on something. These are coarse comparisons to make with such a precious gift, but I can't think of any others.

In this state of prayer, the soul has so much joy it forgets about itself and everything else. Its joy causes it to neither think nor speak of anything but God's praise. Let us all join with this soul in praise, my daughters, for why do we want to appear wiser? And what can make us happier? May all creatures unite their praise with ours forever and ever. Amen, amen, amen!

Seven

Sorrow for Sin

It might seem to you, sisters, that souls who have received God's special communications are so sure of their eternity with Him that they no longer fear or mourn over past sins. But if you hold this opinion then you have never received these special favors. If you have received them, then you know what I am about to say.

The fact is sorrow for sin increases in proportion to the divine blessings we receive. And I do not believe this sorrow will ever leave us until we come to the land where we can grieve no more.

As we progress, I believe we feel this sorrow differently. A soul deep in the Castle no longer suffers thinking about the punishment we justly deserve for our sins. Instead, this soul regrets how ungrateful it has been to Him whom it owes so much and who deserves to be served. Because this soul has been taught divine mysteries, it better understands the greatness of God.

This soul can't believe how bold and irreverent it has been. Its past foolishness seems like madness. It can't stop feeling regret as it remembers the terrible things it pursued while it rejected the great King. Thoughts dwell on this more than on the favors received. The sorrow is so powerful that it seems to rush through the soul like a swift, strong river. And the burden of this sorrow remains like mud in the riverbed.

I know someone who no longer wished for death to see God but wished for death to free her from the regret she carried for her ingratitude. She realized how much she owed Him and would always owe Him. She believed no one's guilt could be as great as hers, and no one could have received as much patience and kindness from Him.

Souls who reach this deep Mansion no longer fear hell. Rarely do they grieve about the possibility of losing God. Their only fear is that He will withdraw His hand, removing His protection so they return to their previous miserable condition and offend Him. They do not care about their reputation or suffering. If they are anxious about spending time in purgatory it is not because of the agony, but because they will be kept from God.

No matter what favors a soul has received from God, it is dangerous to forget the miserable condition it was once in. This memory is beneficial, despite the pain that it brings.

Perhaps I can't forget my sins because of how great they have been. Perhaps people who lead better lives have less sorrow, but we all sin while we are in this human body. Even when we remember our Lord has forgiven and forgotten our faults, the regret remains. And our sorrow increases when we who deserve condemnation receive His kindness and blessings.

I think Saint Paul and Mary Magdalen must have suffered cruelly. Their love was intense, and they witnessed firsthand the majesty of God. The many mercies they received from Jesus must have made the memory of their past sin very painful. Their regret must have filled them with deep sorrow.

Meditations on the Humanity of Christ

You may think that someone who has enjoyed these high blessings (such as raptures and the prayer of quiet) are so absorbed in their love for God that they no longer need to meditate on the mysteries of the humanity of our Lord Jesus Christ. When I previously wrote about this topic, I was told I was wrong, and I did not understand. I was told that as a soul progresses, the Lord guides it to focus on the Father in heaven, not God's humanity in Christ. But nothing can make me believe this is true.

I may be mistaken – perhaps we are all saying the same thing. But I discovered the devil was trying to deceive me about this. So based on my experience, I have decided to speak out about it again. Be cautious about this subject. Listen to what I say, and do not believe anyone who tells you differently. I will try to explain it more clearly this time. It would be helpful for people who write on these matters to be clearer because speaking in general terms can mislead less educated people.

Some people tell us we should not meditate on Christ's final days, and on the lives of the blessed Virgin and the saints. But the example of these lives greatly benefits and strengthens us. If this is true, then what are people supposed to meditate on? Are we supposed to stop thinking about all human things? This is not possible while we are in human flesh.

We are not like angelic spirits who are always filled with love. We need to study, consider, and imitate people who have performed great things for God. And even more so, we should think about our Salvation, the most sacred humanity of our Lord Jesus Christ. Anyone who avoids these topics (and I believe they can't be avoided), misunderstands their minds and harms themselves and others.

I tell them this with certainty: They will never find the way to the last two Mansions if they lose our Guide, our good Jesus. And they may not be safe in the earlier Mansions, either. Our Lord Himself tells us He is the way and the light, and that no one comes to the Father but through Him. And He says, "He that sees Me, sees the Father."[66] These people tell us Jesus' words have another meaning. I do not see any other meaning except the one that my soul recognizes as true.

Some people who were brought by our Lord to perfect contemplation through spiritual favors (and who spoke to me on this subject), want to enjoy this experience continually. This is impossible. Yet the grace of this experience remains with them so that they can't meditate as before on the life and death of Christ.

I do not know the reason, but this inability is common. I think it is because meditation seeks God through the work of the intellect. Once He has been found, these souls become accustomed to seeking God through the will, which is full of love. Since this is much easier, it no longer wearies itself by searching for Him through the intellect.

I can understand that if the will is full of love for God, then reason is unnecessary. But this is impossible for souls who have not reached the last two Mansions. The will is not

[66] John 8:12, 9, 14:6

enough. Reason is still necessary to rekindle love, and prayer without reason is ineffective.

Pay attention to this point, sisters. It is so important I will explain it more. A soul who only wants to spend time loving God and doing nothing else may find the flame of love in the will dies if the spark is not fanned. Should the soul wait for the fire from heaven to consume it with love, like Elijah waited for the fire to consume his sacrifice?[67] Certainly not. And it is not right to expect miracles. God decides when He will work miracles in the soul.

As I have already said and will say again, His Majesty wants us to have an attitude of humility. He also wants us to help ourselves to the best of our abilities and not wait for miracles. In my opinion, this is how we should behave our entire lives, no matter how amazing our prayers may be.

True, those whom our Lord allows into the seventh Mansion may have a burning love that never subsides. When I write about the final Mansion, you will understand that these souls are constantly in the company of Christ our Lord – both in His humanity and His divinity.

But if the fire in our will is burned out or if we do not feel the presence of God, we must search for Him like the bride in the Song of Solomon.[68] We must ask all creatures "who it was that made them," as Saint Augustine tells us he did in his search for God.

We should not foolishly waste our time waiting for

---

[67] 1 Kings 18:30-39
[68] Song of Solomon 3:1-3

spiritual favors given in the past. His Majesty may give us these favors again in a year or in many years. Only His Majesty knows the reason for delay, and there is no reason for us to know or desire to know.

Since we know the way to please God is by keeping His commandments and teachings, then let us do this diligently. Meditate on His life and death and all we owe Him. Then let God choose the rest.

Some may say that after receiving these spiritual favors, their minds can't concentrate on the mysteries of the humanity of our Lord Jesus Christ for reasons we already covered. To a certain extent this might be true. But there is a difference between remembering truths and using your reason to understand truths. Maybe you do not understand, so let me try my best to explain.

Using your reason to understand truths is what I call meditation. For example, think about the mercy God has shown by giving us His only Son. But do not stop there – consider all the mysteries of His glorious life. Or turn your thoughts to His prayer in the garden and follow Him to the crucifixion. Think about a moment in the Passion, such as Christ's arrest. Consider in detail every aspect such as the betrayal of Judas, the scattering of the apostles, and all that followed. This is an admirable and beneficial meditation.

It is true that souls led by God in supernatural ways that practice perfect contemplation can't practice this type of meditation. I do not know why, but as a rule they are unable. But it is impossible for a soul who has received so much from God to forget these precious proofs of His love, especially when our Church celebrates them. These are living sparks that rekindle the heart with greater love for our Lord. And the mind can never fully understand these mysteries.

Because of how they are recalled and stamped in the memory, souls who have attained a higher state of prayer understand these mysteries in a more perfect way than other people. Just looking at a picture of our Lord kneeling in the garden covered by that terrible sweat is enough to occupy their thoughts for not just an hour, but days. A single gaze by these souls on Him is enough to remind them how ungrateful they are for His terrible sufferings. And then the will responds with the simple desire to serve Him and suffer for Him who has borne so much for us. Our memory and understanding then join with the will in considering how to respond.

I think that because these souls can respond with little prompting, they think they are unable to meditate on the Passion of our Lord. But those who have difficulty meditating should still practice remembering these truths. This won't prevent higher prayer and it is good to often remember Him.

If someone is engaged in a meditation on the humanity of Christ and God decides to suspend their intellect, then that is well and good. And even if the soul does not want this, God will make it abandon what it was thinking about, and it will be good for the soul. I still believe that people who have achieved a higher state of prayer will struggle with this type of meditation. But just because this is what usually happens, God still may lead souls in different ways.

So let us not judge those who are unable to meditate on Christ's humanity because they have experienced higher prayer, or judge those who seem incapable of enjoying the mysteries of higher prayer. But no one, however spiritual they may be, can convince me we should ever turn away from God's humanity in Christ.

Some souls think it is a great thing to enjoy these higher spiritual pleasures continually in a state of "absorption" as they experience the sweetness and consolation of the prayer of the quiet. As I have advised elsewhere, stop being so spiritually consumed. Life is long and full of crosses. We need to look at Christ as our example. See how He bore our trials. And see the example of His apostles and saints so we can bear our trials perfectly.

The company of our good Jesus and His blessed Mother is too good to be missed. He is pleased when we grieve about His suffering, even at the cost of our own consolation and joy. Besides, we can't have endless consolation in prayer. And I do not believe anyone who says they do.

Be certain of this: Stay away from this deception. Do all that is in your power to stop yourself from being constantly immersed in this intoxication. If you can't, tell the prioress so she can give you a task to keep you busy. Then you will be free of the danger of hurting your health and mind.

I believe I have given enough proof to those who need it. However spiritual you are, you still live in the world. Do not believe that meditation on the most sacred humanity of Christ can injure the soul.

In defense, people say that our Lord told His disciples that it was better for them if He left because His humanity was less important than the Spirit who followed.[69] I do not agree with this interpretation. I would wager that our Lord did not tell His own blessed Mother that it would be better for her if He left! She had strong faith and knew He was both God and man. She loved Him so perfectly that His presence was more of a help than a hindrance. When Jesus told His disciples this, it must have been to help them since they were not as firm in their faith as they were later. Those of us alive now have reason to have stronger faith.

I assure you, daughters, this interpretation is dangerous. The devil might use it to rob us of our devotion to the most blessed sacrament of communion. I did not go that far when I was mistaken about this, but I avoided meditating on our Lord Jesus Christ, preferring to remain absorbed in higher prayer, waiting for spiritual consolation. I knew I was going wrong. I could not focus, and my thoughts kept wandering. My soul felt like a bird flying about with no place to rest. I wasted time and did not advance in prayer or virtue. I thought I was acting wisely but did not know why I was not progressing.

Finally, I consulted a servant of God about my method of prayer and found my error. I regret that I thought I would benefit by stopping meditation on Christ's humanity and Passion. Even if I could, I would never again try to gain from anything except that which comes by Him through whom comes all the good we possess. May He be forever praised! Amen.

---

[69] John 16:7

Eight

Y ou see, sisters, what I have told you is true. The more the soul progresses in this Castle, the closer the companionship of Jesus. It is important for me to explain that sometimes when He chooses, there is nothing you can do to withdraw from His presence.

This constant reminder of His presence and love comes through wonderful visions His Majesty uses to communicate with us. If He is pleased to help me, I will describe them for you, so you will not be alarmed if you are granted these favors. And even if you never receive them, praise Him for His power and majesty, and for how He communicates with His creatures.

The Presence of Christ

It can happen that a soul who is not looking for this favor, and never imagined itself worthy of it, becomes suddenly conscious of the presence of Jesus Christ. It becomes aware of Him standing by its side even though it does not see Him with the eyes of its body or soul.

This is an intellectual vision since no images are seen. I know a person to whom God gave this favor and other favors I will describe later. At first it worried her because she did not understand what was happening. She could not see anything, but she was convinced she felt Jesus Christ was there. She was certain that she was experiencing something spiritual, but she was not sure it was coming from God.

The powerful effect of this experience proved a strong confirmation that it was coming from Him. She felt certain of our Lord's presence, and He spoke to her several times. She had never learned about intellectual visions or thought this type of vision was possible. But she clearly recognized His voice. Unlike an imaginative vision, the sense of His immediate presence did not pass quickly. It can last several days and sometimes more than a year.

She was frightened by the experience and went to her spiritual advisor, who asked her to describe what she saw since she was so certain of His presence. But while she was certain it was Him who spoke to her and not a trick of her imagination, she did not see anything. Although her advisor cautioned her to not believe in it, she found it impossible, especially when she heard the words, "It is I, be not afraid." These words were so powerful that from then on she could not doubt the vision.

In His company, she was encouraged and rejoiced. She effortlessly remembered Him throughout her day. The sense that He was by her side watching made her more careful not to displease Him in any way. Whenever she wanted to speak to His Majesty, He seemed so close that it would be impossible for Him not to hear her. And while He did not respond whenever she wished, He did respond when it was not expected, and always when it was important.

It is hard to explain how she was conscious of Him being near her, but not in the same way as an ordinary person. His presence was subtle, yet certain. We might think someone is standing next to us, only to turn and find they are gone. But in this case, the certainty of His presence brought graces and spiritual effects that could not be the result of emotion. And they could not have come from the devil since his work does not bring peace or the constant desire to please God and avoid anything that is against Him. As time went on, the Lord showed her clearly that this intellectual vision was not the work of the evil one.

Despite this, she was often worried and confused. She could not understand why she had received such a high favor. It brought an overwhelming sense of humility. This is more evidence that the vision did not come from Satan, who produces the opposite desire in us. And human effort can't produce humility, either. The soul who receives humility knows it does not come from its good, but from the good gift of God.

Although I think some of the spiritual favors already mentioned may be greater, an intellectual vision like this brings a special knowledge of God. A tender love emerges when you feel constantly in His presence. More than any favor yet described, this vision increases your desire to devote yourself completely to His service.

The knowledge of His ongoing close presence also purifies our minds, for although we know God sees everything we do, our nature causes us to grow careless and forgetful. But when our Lord makes our soul conscious that He is close at hand, it is impossible to forget. This knowledge prepares our souls to receive the other effects mentioned while feeling love for Him who is at our side.

In summary, the benefits brought by this favor prove its

value. Our souls thank our Lord for giving this favor to someone so unworthy but who would refuse to exchange it for any earthly riches or delight. When our Lord chooses to withdraw His vivid presence, the soul in its loneliness makes every effort to ask Him to return. But this grace only comes as He wills, and not by our efforts.

At times, we may enjoy the company of a saint, which is also very beneficial. You may ask, if we can see no one during an intellectual vision, how can we know if it is Christ, or His most glorious Mother, or a saint? It seems easy for the soul to recognize when our Lord speaks. And while our soul can't explain how, it knows with great certainty which saint has been sent by God to be its companion and helper, even without hearing a word.

Many spiritual experiences simply can't be explained. We need to remember that our nature is incapable of understanding the mysteries of God.

Response to this Vision

Those who receive favors like this should marvel and praise God's mercy. Since these experiences are not given to everyone, those who receive them should value them and work harder to serve God since they have been given special aid. These people should not consider themselves special. Rather, they should realize the inadequacy of their service and feel under more obligation to Him than others. Given the circumstances, any fault committed will be felt more deeply.

Any of you blessed by this type of intellectual vision can be certain that it is not imagination or a deception if the effects described are experienced. I believe it is impossible for the devil to produce an illusion that lasts so long, causing such inner peace and benefit to the soul. A creature this evil could not bring about so much good. Instead, the devil has a habit of clouding the soul with self-esteem and the idea that you are better than others. And a mind so continually focused on the presence of God and thoughts about Him would enrage the devil. The devil might experiment with this deception, but he would not return to it.

Remember, God is faithful. He will not give the devil power over someone whose only goal is to please His Majesty and lay down their life for His honor and glory.[70] God will quickly reveal the devil's deception.

I believe – and I always will – that God will gain glory from a soul who reaps the benefits of these divine favors. Therefore, as I told you, daughters, if you receive intellectual visions, you should not be astonished. Fear is good, and we should be cautious. Nor should you be over-confident, since feeling favored can make you careless. If you do not receive the effects mentioned, then it proves these visions are not from God.

If you have an intellectual vision, it would be a good idea to explain your experience to a well-qualified theologian (for this is where you should go to gain understanding) or to some highly spiritual person. It would be best if the spiritual person was also a good theologian. But do not be upset if he says you are imagining things. If true, then this imagination can't harm

---

[70] 1 Corinthians 10:13

or benefit your soul very much. Go to His Majesty and beg Him to prevent your imagination from misleading you.

It would be worse if your advisor told you that the devil is deceiving you with these visions. Anyone with knowledge would realize it could not be the devil because of the effects of the intellectual vision that we have mentioned. But even if your advisor says you are being deceived, the Lord who is beside you will comfort you, assure you, and give your counselor wisdom to share for your benefit.

If, despite prayer, your counselor is not led by God in this way, he will only fear for you and condemn these visions. Therefore, I advise you to choose someone who has studied God's word and if possible, is also spiritual. Your prioress should allow you to consult this person so both of you are sure you are safe from delusion, even if you lead a good life.

After you have met with your advisor, be at peace and do not look for more advice. Do not trouble yourself anymore about your intellectual visions. Sometimes even when there is no reason to fear, the devil makes us unsatisfied with a single opinion, especially if we are inexperienced or timid. And when too many people know, something that was supposed to be private becomes public. You may find you are persecuted and tormented when what was supposed to be secret becomes public knowledge.

This trouble not only creates suffering for the individual but may even affect the Order. I warn all prioresses to be discreet about these situations and not give special treatment to a nun who has received these favors.

Our Lord gives each of us guidance in the way He knows

to be best. An intellectual vision, if made good use of, prepares one to become a great servant of God. But God may also give this gift to the weakest of souls. The person receiving this gift should neither be highly valued nor condemned. Remember, the holy person is the one who is humble, pure, and single-minded in their service to God.

But we can never be certain about these things until the true Judge rewards each person based on what they deserve. That is when we will be surprised to find how different His judgments are from those of the world. May He be praised forever. Amen.

Nine

Imaginative Visions

Now we will talk about *imaginative visions* – visions seen by the eyes of our soul in the form of images – which I believe the devil uses to deceive people more than any other type of vision I have described thus far. But imaginative visions from God may benefit us more because they are uniquely designed for our nature. Only the visions sent by our Lord in the seventh Mansion surpass all visions, including these.

Let us consider the constant presence of our Lord described in the last chapter. It is as though we have a gold locket containing a precious stone with great value and healing power. Even though we have not seen the stone, we are certain it exists. We feel its power whenever we carry the locket. Although unseen, we prize the stone because it healed us of certain illnesses it was designed to remedy.

But we can never open the locket and look at the precious stone, because only the owner of the jewel knows the secret to opening the locket. Although the jewel has been lent to us for our benefit, the owner keeps the key for himself. He will only open the locket when he decides, and he may take back the jewel whenever he wishes.

Now suppose that the owner of the jewel opens the locket out of kindness toward the locket bearer. Certainly, the locket bearer will value the locket even more after seeing the incredible brilliance of the jewel inside. And the happy memory will stay with them for a very long time.

This story illustrates what happens when our Lord is pleased to delight our souls with an imaginative vision. Like opening the locket, He shows us images of His most sacred humanity on earth or as He is after His resurrection. The vision passes as quickly as a flash of lightning. But the glorious image will not be forgotten until the soul sees Christ at last and enjoys Him forever.

I called this an "image," but you do not see it through your eyes the same way you view a painting. The image of Christ as a living person speaking and even revealing deep mysteries is seen through your interior eyes. Just like it is impossible to gaze long at the sun, this image always passes quickly, but unlike the sun, the brilliance is not painful.

Only our interior eyes see this vision. I can't tell you anything about visions that come from our exterior sight, since I can't be certain about something I have not experienced. But the splendid light of Christ revealed by this interior sight is like that of the sun covered by something sparkling, like a cut diamond. His clothing is like fine Dutch linen.

The soul who receives this vision is almost always overcome in a rapture. Our nature is too weak to bear such a frightful sight. I say "frightful" even though this apparition is more lovely than anything that could be imagined. Even if we were to live a thousand years and spend all that time trying to picture this vision, it surpasses all our imagination and understanding. Yet this unsurpassed majesty also brings great fear to our soul.

It is not necessary to ask how the soul knows, without being told, that this is the Lord of heaven and earth. It knows this with certainty. This does not happen when we see earthly kings. We might not even notice them unless they identify themselves or are accompanied by members of their court.

Oh Lord, how little we Christians know You! Today You come as a friend to Your spouse, and the sight of You overwhelms us with awe. Oh, daughters, what will it be like when He comes as a judge and loudly says, "Depart from me, you who are cursed."[71]

This reminder is a great blessing. Even Saint Jerome, although he was a saint, kept the thought of the last judgment always before his eyes. We must remember that all we suffer now in the strict observance of our religious lives will seem like nothing. For however long it lasts, it is only a moment compared to eternity.

I promise you, as wicked as I am, I have never feared the torments of hell. I realize that before these torments, the lost will see the beautiful, humble, and kind eyes of our Lord turned on them in judgment. This is what I fear. Hell is nothing to me compared to the thought of this look. It would be more than my heart could bear.

If the Lord reveals Himself to you in an imaginative vision, then this experience should give you greater fear of judgment. In an imaginative vision, the Lord reveals Himself so powerfully that the person becomes unconscious. Fear in this

---

[71] Matthew 25:14

moment can only be overcome by a rapture of our soul that engulfs the senses and faculties. Our Lord strengthens our weakness so He can unite His greatness in beautiful communion.

If someone says that during this experience they gazed on the face of the Lord for a long time, then I do not believe it was a true imaginative vision. Rather, it was intense thoughts that caused an active imagination. Compared to a true vision, what they saw was dead.

Since many people have spoken to me about this – and not just two or three or four – I know there are many souls who can visualize anything. Maybe they have active minds or vivid imaginations. But if they ever had a genuine imaginative vision, they would recognize false imaginations immediately.

Some people come up with an image they want to see and then build it in their minds little by little. But this imagining leaves no effect on the mind. No greater devotion comes from this than from looking at a sacred picture. We should not pay attention to these fantasies, which pass more quickly than dreams from the memory.

In a true imaginative vision, it is much different. The vision comes suddenly and completely. The person is not thinking about seeing a vision. The thought is not even on their mind when the entire vision is revealed. The powers and senses of the soul move quickly from confusion and fear to peace and joy.

Remember Saint Paul falling to the ground on the road to

Damascus.[72] A great light came from heaven, but in the interior world of his soul, perfect calm immediately followed his fear and astonishment.

And while all this is happening to the soul, spiritual truths are impressed on the mind. No human effort is needed to gain this wisdom, for it is Wisdom Himself who enlightens ignorance and leaves it certain that this favor is from God.

Doubters

Even if people express their doubts that this grace came from God, the soul is certain. And this certainty lasts a long time. If a spiritual advisor suggests doubt, God may allow faith to waver. The soul might believe it has been deceived because of its sin. But the soul's uncertainty does not last, and it does not give in to doubts.

The devil's temptations in this Mansion only disturb the mind. In fact, when the attacks of doubt are severe, the soul is more certain that its imaginative vision came from God. The evil one has no power over the interior of the soul, so he can never produce the spiritual blessing of the vision. The deceiver can never possess truth, majesty, and power.

If a spiritual advisor cannot see the spiritual effects on the soul, they suspect the imaginative vision is a deception. Perhaps the soul tried but failed to give a good explanation of the effects it is experiencing. Spiritual advisors should be patient and wait to see what effects follow before passing judgment. They should watch for increased humility and

---

[72] Acts 9:3-4

virtue. But if the devil is involved, he will soon show signs of himself and be detected in a thousand lies.

If the spiritual advisor has received imaginative visions themselves, or has the gift of discerning spirits, then it will not take long to discover the truth. In fact, they will know immediately upon hearing about the vision whether it came from God, the devil, or the imagination.

The point is, sisters, you should be perfectly open and honest with your spiritual advisors. Of course, you should be open and honest when you confess your sins, but this is not what I am talking about. I am saying you should be perfectly truthful in giving an account of your prayers and visions. If you do not do this, then I can't assure you of your safety, or that you are led by God.

Our Lord wants us to be truthful with Him and those who stand in His place. We should want our spiritual advisors to know all thoughts and actions that result from these visions, even if they seem insignificant. If you are truthful, there is no reason to feel troubled or worried.

Even if the vision is not from God, if you are humble and have a good conscience, it will do you no harm. In these cases, His Majesty knows how to draw good from evil. Believing the devil's deception that God gave you these imaginative visions may cause you to work harder to please God and stay focused on Him. The devil's intention to injure you instead becomes your benefit.

A great teacher once said that the devil is a clever painter. But if the devil presented him with a living image of Christ, the teacher would not be troubled. The image would only make him more devoted, defeating the evil one with his very weapons.

No matter how poor the artist, we should cherish his paintings if they represent Him who is our only good. This same teacher thought we should never doubt someone who says they have seen a vision of our Lord. Whenever we see a portrait of our King, we should show it respect. I am sure he is right! We would be offended if someone treated our own portrait with contempt. How much more should we show respect to a crucifix or a picture of our heavenly King wherever it meets our gaze!

I have written about this topic before, and I am glad I can teach about it again. It is upsetting when people doubt that God gives visions. I know a spiritual advisor who in his ignorance advised making an obscene gesture if an imaginative vision ever came upon them. Since he believed visions were not possibly from God, this was supposed to break the habit.

It would be painful to be told to behave this way, and torturous to feel you must obey your superior. We are led to believe our soul could be lost if we disobey. If you are given this order, I advise you not to obey. Humbly explain the reasons I have given you, which follow the advice of the great teacher I mention.

Warnings

One great advantage of an imaginative vision is that its fruit is lasting. You may be thinking about Christ's life and Passion when the memory of your vision of His meek and beautiful face returns. It is like the feeling we have coming face to face with someone who has been very good to us. Remembering the joy of imaginative visions gives great comfort and strength.

Many other benefits come from receiving imaginative visions. I have written about this elsewhere and will continue this subject in the final Mansion. I will say no more here so you and I do not grow weary.

But I need to give you strong advice. Do not pray or desire the favor of an imaginative vision. You may hear of God giving this grace to others, and it might appear very good to you. You may believe someone who receives them should be highly esteemed. But there are many reasons you should not seek imaginative visions.

First, if you want something you do not deserve, it shows a lack of humility. I do not think anyone who longs for these graces can really be humble. A common worker never dreams of becoming a king. Not only is it impossible, but he is also not even fit to be a king.

A humble person feels the same way about these divine favors. If God has given them self-knowledge, then they know they are not worthy. A person who expects this favor forgets His great mercy in saving them from the condemnation they deserve.

Second, a person who wants this grace is in great danger of the devil's deception. He only needs to see the door left slightly open to slip in and play a thousand tricks.

Third, when a person wants something badly, their imagination causes them to believe they have seen something they have not. A mind set on something all day dreams about it at night.

Fourth, if we do not know what is good for us, it would be arrogant for us to hope we should receive imaginative visions. We should yield to our Lord, Who knows our souls, and trust Him to guide us in the best way so His will may be done.

Fifth, do you think people who receive these favors from our Lord do not suffer? They absolutely suffer! They experience many severe trials. How do you know if you could bear them?

Sixth, what you think is gain can become loss. Remember what happened to Saul when he was made king.

Sisters, there are many more reasons I have not mentioned. Believe me, it is safer to wish for only what God wishes for. He loves us and knows us better than we know ourselves. Let us place ourselves entirely in His hands, so that His will may be done in us. We can never go astray if our will is fixed on this.

Receiving these favors will not earn you greater glory. Since you have received more, your debt to God increases. There are many holy people who never received imaginative visions, and many unholy people who have.

And do not think that this blessing is continually given. Each time you receive an imaginative vision, the soul bears many trials. Thus, the soul does not strive to receive more imaginative visions but focuses on how to serve in return for what it has received.

True imaginative visions can be a powerful aid in helping us practice more perfect virtue. But a person who gains more perfect virtue with the cost of their own labor is more commendable.

I knew two people (one was a man) who received imaginative visions from God. The memory of them brought both great comforts. But both would rather have served His Majesty without the benefit of those memories. They wanted to bear the full cost of their service and suffer for His sake.

For that reason, if it had been possible, they would have refused these visions. But, of course, they understood that the imaginative vision greatly benefits the soul and is to be highly valued.

I believe desires like this are supernatural. They come from souls inflamed with love for God. It is good to want to prove to God that you serve Him for more reasons than receiving His blessings. You should want to work hard to satisfy your love for Him, not to gain personal glory. People who feel this desire to show their love in a thousand ways. If possible, they want love to consume their soul. If God could gain greater glory, they would offer the destruction of their soul and count it a blessing.

May He be praised forever! In lowering Himself to speak with us miserable creatures, He promises to reveal His greatness! Amen.

Ten

There are many reasons our Lord communicates with souls through visions in the sixth Mansion. Sometimes, He communicates when we are suffering or are about to receive a heavy cross. Other times it is just for the mutual delight of Himself and His beloved.

It is not my goal to describe every reason He may communicate with us. I want to teach you (as well as I know how) about the characteristics and effects of these favors so you will be able to identify what is merely your imagination.

If you see a true vision, you will know these visions are possible and this knowledge will prevent you from becoming frightened by the experience. The devil is delighted when he sees a soul troubled and distressed. He knows this prevents it from fully loving and serving God.

His Majesty has higher ways of communicating with the soul, and I will explain two of them now. These are less dangerous because I do not think evil spirits can imitate them. But they are also more mysterious and harder to explain than imaginative visions.

Vision of God Over All

In this first higher vision, the soul may be praying normally when God is pleased to suddenly suspend its senses. In that moment, sublime mysteries are revealed. It seems like the soul sees God Himself, since this is not a vision of Christ as a man.

The soul actually "sees" nothing. This is not an imaginative vision but an intellectual vision, since no images are seen. In the moment it receives this vision, the soul immediately receives the knowledge that all things are seen by God and contained by God.

This favor is very beneficial. Although it passes in an instant, it leaves a deep impression on the memory. The soul feels shame as it understands its worst sins have been committed right in front of Him. Nothing is hidden. Even though we have been taught this and it seems obvious, it is as though we never understood it until now. Perhaps this is because we never wanted to understand the implications. If we did, how could we behave with such boldness?

I will try to explain this truth with a comparison. Let us imagine God to be a spacious and magnificent palace. Do you think a sinner living in this palace can escape to carry out his crimes? It is impossible. The world is His palace. So all our sinful and shameful thoughts and actions are committed right in front of Him. This awful truth is worth our meditation! How can we be so reckless?

Sisters, think about the infinite mercy and patience of God. Let us thank Him for not casting us immediately to hell. When we recognize our flagrant sin in the presence of God our Creator, we should be ashamed of resenting anything said or done to us by others. Yet when we hear of one unkind word spoken behind our backs – even with no evil intention – we are completely wounded. Oh, misery of mankind!

When, daughters, will we ever imitate the Almighty God? Stop thinking you are doing great things when you become impatient in suffering injury. We must welcome this injury. Let us love our enemies, since this great God has not stopped loving us despite our many sins! This is the main reason we must forgive each other.

I assure you, daughters, that though this type of vision passes quickly, our Lord has bestowed a great grace on those who keep the memory constantly in mind.

Vision of God as Truth

Like the previous higher vision, this second one also only lasts a moment. While it is impossible to describe, suddenly God reveals to the soul that in Him alone there is truth. This truth overshadows any truth in humankind. He convinces the soul that He alone is the Truth, unable to lie.

David's words in the psalm, "Everyone is a liar," are for the first time clear. [73] No matter how often we have heard that God's word is true, we only fully understand it in this moment.

I remember reading Pilate's question to our Lord, "What is truth?"[74] I realize how little we understand here below about this supreme Truth. I wish I had the ability to explain this better. Sisters, let us learn from this. If we want to bear any resemblance to our God and Spouse, we must always walk in this truth.

And I do not only mean that you should tell God the truth. In our convents you are careful to do this. But I wish that as much as possible you walk in truth with both God and man.

[73] Psalm 116:11
[74] John 18:36-38

We should not wish people thought better of us than we are. In our works we should credit God for what is His and credit ourselves for what is ours. But we need to do this honestly. When we do this, the world – which is only temporary deception and lies – will lose its power over us.

I was once wondering why our Lord so dearly loves humility, and I was struck by a thought. Our Lord loves humility because God is the supreme Truth, and humility is the truth. The truth is, we have nothing good within ourselves, only misery and emptiness. If you do not accept this, then you live a lie. If you accept this, then you are pleasing to God, the supreme Truth, because you are walking in the truth.[75] Sisters, may God give us the grace to never lose this self-knowledge! Amen.

Our Lord shows the soul these favors because it is now indeed His bride. As His bride, the soul commits to doing His will in all things. And He wishes to help it do this so it may become more like Him.

I do not need to add any more to what I have said. I believe learning about these two higher visions will prove useful to you. There is nothing to fear in receiving these favors. Rather, He should be praised for granting them. And the soul may rest in peace knowing that neither the devil nor our imagination can have much to do with them.

---

[75] 1 John 1:6-7

Eleven

Do you remember the little dove and butterfly? Will these favors given by the Spouse be enough to bring contentment? Will they be able to settle down and rest in the place where they are to die?

No, indeed, their condition is worse than ever. For even though they have received these favors for years, each grace makes the pain worse. They still feel far away from God. As they learn more about Him, their longing and love grow stronger. They realize how this great God and King deserves to be fully loved.

Over the years as its love for Him grows stronger, the soul experiences the bitter suffering I am about to describe. I say "years" because that was the experience of someone I know. But I know God has no time limits and can raise a soul to a higher level in a single moment. His Majesty has the power to do all He wishes, and He wishes to do a lot for us.

As a result of our love for Him we experience longings, tears, sighs, and strong and sudden desires. But compared to the painful fire I am about to describe, these are only smoldering embers.

The Dart

While the soul is in this condition longing for God, a passing thought or comment may remind it that death is still far away. This sudden unwelcome thought comes like a blow from a fiery dart. Of course, there is no actual dart, but the soul realizes the feeling could not come about naturally.

No physical blow or pain is inflicted, but a severe wound is felt in the very depths and center of the soul. Like a thunderbolt, this dart seems to turn the body to dust. In the instant this occurs there is not even a memory of our being. The faculties of the soul become paralyzed so the only power it has is to intensify the pain. Do not think I am exaggerating. I am struggling to explain what can't be described. Somehow the only senses and faculties not held in a trance are those that increase the agony.

The mind becomes sharply aware of the grief caused by our separation from God. And His Majesty adds to this sorrow by vividly making the soul aware of His presence. This increases the agony to such a degree that the sufferer lets out loud cries that can't be stifled. Since this pain attacks the innermost place in the soul, even one accustomed to pain can't stop from crying out.

What we learn from this is that the soul is capable of much greater suffering than the body. We better understand the suffering of hell. Just because the body is absent does not mean that the torture of hell will be easier than our bodily suffering in this world.

I once saw someone in this condition, and I really thought they would die. This should not come as a shock, because there is great danger of death in this situation. Even though this suffering of the soul lasts only a short time, it leaves the limbs disjointed and the pulse feeble. Indeed, the body grows colder, as if the soul is on the point of departure. If there was any increase in the supernatural burning in the soul, God would satisfy the soul's desire for death to be with Him.

As I have said, no bodily pain is felt in the moment. But for two or three days afterward, the joints feel like they have been dislocated. One can ache so much that one does not have the strength to hold a pen. Indeed, I think the body never completely recovers from this experience.

Bodily pain is not felt during the experience because it is overshadowed in the moment by spiritual pain. It is similar to how a great pain in one area of our body prevents us from noticing an ache somewhere else. The spiritual pain is so intense that any physical pain goes unnoticed. I do not think you would be aware of your physical pain even if you were being cut to pieces.

You may think that someone who experiences this dart – the reminder that death is still far away – must be spiritually immature. Perhaps this person has not completely surrendered themselves to the will of God. They should accept that their time on earth is not yet over.

But this is not the case. Up until this moment, the soul had dedicated its life to becoming more surrendered to God's will. But when it receives this dart, the soul can't control its reasoning any longer. It can only think about the reason for its grief. It feels separated from its only Good and wonders why it must continue to live.

The soul feels a strange loneliness. No companion can be found on earth or in heaven since they are not the Beloved. It is like someone suspended in mid-air, unable to touch the ground or reach the heavens. The soul is thirsty but can't reach the water. It is a thirst that can't be quenched. Only the true water our Lord spoke of to the Samaritan woman will do, but this has not been given.[76]

Alas, oh Lord, to what a state You bring those who love You! Yet these sufferings are nothing compared to the reward You give them. It is right that great riches should be costly.

Most important, as purgatory cleanses spirits to enter heaven, this suffering purifies the soul so it may enter the seventh Mansion. When we reach that place, these trials will seem like a drop of water in the sea.

I believe the suffering and grief of this experience is greater than any earthly trial – and I have endured many trials in both body and mind. But compared with the benefits of this experience, the suffering is nothing. The soul realizes it does not deserve such a great favor.

Knowing the suffering is for its own good does not bring the soul relief, but it does help it bear future suffering willingly. And if God desires it, the soul is willing to accept trials that last a lifetime. Truly, instead of dying once, this would be a living death.

Let us remember, sisters, how those who are in hell lack submission to the divine will. They lack the peace and consolation God gives souls who know that blessing comes from their suffering. As we have learned, the soul feels pain more keenly than the body.

But the torments I have just described will be far less than those endured by the lost, who know their anguish will last forever. What will become of these miserable souls? Nothing

---

[76] John 4:7-14

we suffer in this short life will be difficult if it frees us from such terrible and endless torture.

Unless you have learned from experience, it is impossible to explain the intensity of spiritual suffering and how different it is from physical suffering. Our Lord wants us to understand this, so we realize the great debt we owe Him. For through His mercy, He is calling us to the hope of freedom and forgiveness of sin.

Let us return to the soul we left in great torment from this sudden dart. This agony never lasts more than three or four hours. If longer, our weak natures could only endure by a miracle.

In one person's experience, it only lasted fifteen minutes, but the attack was so violent she lost consciousness and was left completely exhausted. It happened during Eastertide when she was going through such a spiritually dry time that she was hardly aware of the observances. On the last day of Easter, she was having a conversation, and a verse about how life can seem unending triggered this experience.

In the same way that we can't prevent being burned if we are thrown into a fire, it is impossible to resist the sudden pain of this experience. It is also impossible to hide what you are feeling. Everyone around you knows you are in a dangerous condition, but they can't understand what is happening to you. During the experience we are aware that our friends are near, but they and all earthly things seem to be in shadows.

If you ever have this experience, know that the weakness of your human nature can come to your aid. Sometimes when a person is dying from her desire for death, the mind fights back. The desire for death fills the soul with so much grief it is ready to leave the body. But the mind is terrified at the thought and tries to calm the pain to hold off death. This saving fear comes from our human weakness.

But the soul's longing for death can't be stilled until God brings it comfort. He may do this by suspending the soul in a trance. Or He may send a vision during which the true Comforter consoles and strengthens the heart's desire to live as long as He wills it.

This spiritual favor comes with great suffering but leaves precious graces within the soul. The soul loses all fear of trials that may be ahead. Compared to the suffering experienced by the soul, anything else it may go through seems insignificant.

Recognizing what was gained, the sufferer would gladly endure the pain again. But she can do nothing about this desire since this experience only comes from God. And when God does allow it again, resistance and escape are impossible.

From this experience the mind feels even more contempt for the world than it had before. It realizes that nothing on earth can satisfy its longing. And it has less expectation of other people, having learned that only its Creator can bring comfort and strength. The mind is more concerned and careful not to offend God, recognizing He can torment as well as comfort.

In this spiritual experience, two things can put your life in danger. The first is the pain of which I have spoken, for this is truly a danger. The second is the overwhelming joy and delight that reaches such a peak the soul seems on the point of leaving the body, something which would bring it even more happiness.

Now you see, sisters, why I told you courage was needed for the spiritual favors in the sixth Mansion. If someone asks for these favors, our Lord may reply as He did to the sons of Zebedee: "Can you drink the cup I am going to drink?"[77]

I believe, sisters, we should all answer "yes." And this is the right answer because His Majesty will give us strength as we need it. As He did for Mary Magdalen, He always defends souls when they are persecuted and slandered, if not in words, then in deeds.[78]

And in the end, before they die, He repays them for all they have suffered, as you shall learn next. May He be forever blessed and may all creatures praise Him! Amen.

---

[77] Matthew 20:22
[78] Luke 7:36-48

The Seventh Mansion

One

You may think, sisters, that so much has been said about our spiritual journey that nothing remains to be said. Such a thought is foolish. God's greatness has no limits, and neither do His works. Who can tell about all His mercies and greatness? It is impossible. So, do not be amazed by what is said and what will be said, for it is nothing compared to what is left to tell of Him.

He has shown us great mercy by communicating with those who can teach us. The more we learn about His communication to creatures, the more we will praise Him and make an effort to think highly of the souls in which He so delights. Each of us possesses a soul, but even though we are creatures made in the image of God, we do not appreciate our soul's value or understand the important secrets it contains.

May His Majesty guide my pen and teach me to say something about what He reveals to souls He leads into this final Mansion. I have begged Him desperately to help me. He knows my goal is to reveal His mercies for the praise and glory of His name.

I hope He will grant this favor, if not for my sake, then at least for yours. I hope you will discover how important it is that you put nothing in the way of the spiritual marriage of the Spouse with your soul, since this marriage brings so many blessings, as you will see.

Oh, great God! Someone as miserable as me is afraid to speak about a subject I do not deserve to understand. I have been so perplexed and believe it might be better to write only a few words about this final Mansion. People may think I am sharing my personal experience if I write more. Knowing who I am, I feel ashamed of trying to take this on. On the other hand, neglecting this Mansion seems like a temptation and a weakness on my part. If God can be better known and praised, let people misjudge and attack me. Besides, I may be dead before this book is ever read. May He be blessed who lives forever! Amen.

Union in the Seventh Mansion

Our Lord desires to finally take pity on the past and present suffering endured by the soul's longing for Him. In the sixth Mansion He spiritually takes the soul for His bride. But before this marriage is consummated in heaven, He brings it into this seventh Mansion, where He is present.

Just as He has a dwelling place in heaven, He has one in the soul, where only He lives. This is the seventh Mansion. It can be called a second heaven.

It is important, sisters, not to imagine the soul as dark even though we can't imagine light inside like we experience outside. It is true a soul can be in darkness when it is not in grace, as was the case in the first Mansion. But this darkness is because the soul is incapable of receiving light from the Sun of Justice who dwells within, giving it being. It is as though these unfortunate souls are imprisoned in a gloomy dungeon. They are blind, dumb, and chained so they are unable to do any good. We should pity them only after we remember we were once in the same state until God showed us mercy, which He may also have on them.

Sisters, let us be diligent to pray for them, since this is a generous act of charity. Suppose we saw a soul tied to a post with his hands behind his back, dying of hunger. All around him is delicious food, but he is unable to put any of it in his mouth. He is exhausted and at the point of dying not a temporary death, but an eternal one. It would be cruel to stand there looking at him and not give him anything to eat. What if your prayers could release his bonds? The answer is obvious. For the love of God, I beg you to constantly remember these souls in prayer.

But now we are talking about souls who, by the mercy of God, have repented and are in a state of grace. Remember, our souls are large and spacious. We are not reflecting on something restricted to a corner but on an interior world containing Mansions with many beautiful rooms, as you have seen. It is right that the soul is like this because at the center there is a Mansion reserved for God Himself.

When His Majesty is ready to grant the soul union through divine marriage, He brings it to this seventh Mansion where He is present. He wants this favor to be different than unions through raptures or the prayer of union experienced in other Mansions. During these unions, the soul does not feel called to its center but to a higher part of the soul. But whether it comes one way or another, I believe our Lord is uniting the soul to Himself.

During raptures and the prayer of union, He makes the soul dumb and blind while it is experiencing the favor, like

Saint Paul during his conversion.[79] The soul does not understand what is happening since the power of its faculties are entirely lost, but it enjoys supreme delight in being near to God.

However, in the seventh Mansion, the soul's union with God comes about in a different way. Our good God now desires to remove the scales from our eyes, letting the soul see and understand the favor being granted.

When the soul is brought into this Mansion, the truth of all three Persons of the Blessed Trinity is revealed through an intellectual vision. First, there comes a radiance in the spirit in the manner of a cloud of magnificent splendor, and then the three Persons are revealed distinctly from one another. Somehow certainty is infused in the soul about the profound truth that all three Persons are one God in substance, power, and knowledge.

Our doctrine of faith, which we speak, is now understood by the soul with sight. The sight, of course, does not come from our eyes or the eyes of our soul since this is not an imaginative vision. All three Persons speak to the soul and make it understand the words of our Lord in the Gospel, that He and the Father and the Holy Spirit will come and make their home in the soul who loves Him and keeps His commandments.[80]

Oh, God, help me! How different it is to understand truth this way, rather than only by hearing and believing these

---

[79] Acts 9:8
[80] John 14:23

words! Day by day a growing astonishment overtakes the soul. The three Persons of the Blessed Trinity never seem to leave it. Even though the soul can't understand or explain it, the soul knows Their companionship in some place very deep within itself.

You may think a soul becomes so preoccupied with the experience that it is unable to care about anything else. But this is not true. Instead, the soul becomes more preoccupied with everything having to do with service to God. Only when it rests does the soul enjoy this blessed companionship.

In my opinion, unless the soul fails God, He will never stop making it aware of His presence. The soul feels confident – as indeed it should – that now that He has given this gift of His presence, He will not allow the soul to lose it. But at the same time, the soul is more careful to avoid disappointing Him in any way.

His presence is not always felt as intensely as it is the first time the soul experiences this favor, or when God renews this favor. If His presence were always felt this fully, the soul would find it impossible to attend to anything else or engage in regular activities.

On most days when His presence is not sensed as clearly, it only takes remembering Him to feel the immediate companionship of the Blessed Trinity. It is like being in a well-lit room full of people when someone closes the shutters so the light to see others is gone. But while we can't see the people again until the light returns, we are certain they are still there.

You might ask if there is anything a soul can do to bring

back the light of companionship, but this is not within its power. Only when the Lord chooses will He open the shutters – the windows of the intellect – to see Him again. Great is His mercy in reassuring us He will always be with us.

It seems that through this divine companionship, His Majesty wants to prepare His bride for greater things. Clearly, the soul is helped in every way to advance in perfection. It loses the fear it once had when other spiritual favors were given.

A certain person who received this favor found she improved in many virtues. No matter what her trials or business affairs, the center of her soul never seemed to move from that room. As a result, it seemed to her that her soul was divided. A short time later she suffered some great trials and complained about the center of her soul like Martha complained about Mary. She was like Martha, dealing with all the trouble and worry, while her soul, like Mary, kept peace with Christ.[81]

Maybe this seems foolish to you, daughters, but it truly happens this way. While we only have one soul, it is common for it to seem divided. Interior effects show us for certain that there is a difference between the soul and the spirit, even though they are one. The difference is very subtle. But sometimes there are differences in their behavior and the knowledge each receives from God.

It also seems to me that the soul and our faculties are separate. But there are so many mysteries about us it would

---

[81] Luke 10:40

be presumptuous for me to try to explain them. If by God's mercy He brings us to heaven, we will someday understand these secrets.

Two

Spiritual Marriage

As I have explained, the divine and spiritual marriage of the seventh Mansion is different than the spiritual unions in other Mansions. While this great favor does not come to perfect fullness while we live, if we forsake God now, we lose this great good forever.

His Majesty wants the soul to understand the sovereign gift of spiritual marriage it is receiving in the seventh Mansion. When God gives this grace, He desires to reveal Himself to the soul through a vison of Christ in His most sacred human form. Others may receive this favor in another way. Once, after receiving Holy Communion, a person saw our Lord in the form of shining splendor, beauty, and majesty as He was after His resurrection. He told her that it was now time for her to own what belonged to Him and that He would take care of what was hers. He spoke other words, too, which she was to hear but not mention.

Because our Lord had revealed Himself to her at other times, this may seem like nothing new. But this experience was so different that it left her confused and frightened. First, because of the force of His words and what He said to her. And second, like the vision described earlier, He revealed Himself and spoke these words to her in the interior part of her soul.

Understand, there is a great difference between visions received in the seventh Mansion in spiritual marriage and those received in any of the other Mansions. It is like the difference in experiences shared by people who are engaged and those unified forever in holy matrimony. I am making this comparison because I can't find another but remember that spiritual marriage has nothing to do with our bodies.

What is true of spiritual marriage is that this secret union takes place in the innermost center of our soul where God Himself must dwell. To enter this place, I do not believe you must go through a door. What I mean is that all the favors I have described thus far pass through or take place through our senses and faculties. But the union in spiritual marriage occurs differently. Here, God appears directly in our soul's center, without passing through anything.

This favor is not an imaginative vision but an intellectual vision more delicate than those mentioned before. It is like the way Jesus appeared to the apostles in the upper room without entering through the door, saying, "Peace be with you."[82] What God communicates to the soul in an instant is great and mysterious, and the soul experiences supreme delight. I can find no comparison. I can only say that the Lord is revealing in that moment, in a more sublime way than in any other vision or spiritual delight, the glory of heaven.

As far as we can understand, the soul – and I mean the spirit of the soul – is made one with God, who is Himself a Spirit. By giving some people this experience, God shows the height to which His love reaches so that we may praise His greatness. Because of His love, He wants to join Himself to

---

[82] John 20:19-21

His creatures so that, just as those who are married can't be separated, He will never separate from the soul.

In the spiritual engagement of the fifth Mansion, God and the soul often separate. The grace of union through raptures or the prayer of union also can be dissolved because even though God and the soul are joined into one, the two can still be separated. We observe this in the prayer of union, which generally passes quickly, and the soul is left without the awareness of His presence.

Unions before the seventh Mansion are like what happens when two wax candles are held closely together. The wicks, wax, and flames become one. But after this union, one candle can easily be separated from the other so there are two candles and two wicks again.

This is not so in spiritual marriage with our Lord: After the union, the soul remains with God in that center. Spiritual marriage is like rain falling from heaven into a river. When they come together, the rainwater can't be separated from the water of the river. Spiritual marriage is like a stream, which upon flowing into an ocean can never again be separated from the ocean. Or it can be compared to a room brightened by the light from two windows. Although the streams of lights are separate, they become one.

Perhaps when Saint Paul said, "He who is joined to the Lord is one in spirit," he was speaking of this spiritual marriage.[83] The same apostle said, "To me, to live is Christ

---

[83] 1 Corinthians 6:17

and to die is gain."[84] This is now the cry of the soul unified in spiritual marriage with Christ. In this Mansion the little butterfly dies with great joy, for Christ is her life.

Peace in the Center

As time goes on, the soul's life in Christ is better understood by the effects on the soul. The soul learns that it is only God who gives it life through secret aspirations too strong to be misunderstood but impossible to describe. The person experiencing these can't hold back loving exclamations they may cause, such as, "Life of my life, and Power that sustains me!"

For from the divine breasts where God seems to sustain the soul come streams of milk that also bring peace to the servants of the Castle. I think He wishes others in the Castle to share the riches enjoyed by the soul. So sometimes drops of water flow to sustain the powers of our body, the servant of the bride and Bridegroom.

Just as a person can't fail to notice if they are suddenly plunged into water, the effects of this union can't go unnoticed. The soul knows with certainty that this great gush of blessing must have a source. It knows that Someone in the interior of the soul is shooting arrows that give it life. And it knows at the center there is a Sun producing a brilliant light that streams to its faculties.

As I have said, the soul in spiritual marriage never moves from this center or loses its peace. For the One who gave

---

[84] Philippians 1:21

peace to His apostles when they were assembled in the upper room gives peace to the soul.[85]

I think this salutation to the apostles has far deeper meaning than the words convey, as well as our Lord's words to Mary Magdalen, "Go in peace."[86] When our Lord speaks, His words are alive and active. They must have worked in those souls, who were trying to rid themselves of the world, to be left pure in spirit.

Only when they were emptied could these souls be joined in spiritual union with the uncreated Spirit. Without a doubt, if – for the love of our Lord – we empty and detach ourselves from all that belongs to the creature, that same Lord will fill us up with Himself.

Thus, our Lord Jesus Christ, praying for His apostles, asked that they might become one with the Father and with Himself, as Jesus and His Father are one.[87] I do not know how love could be greater than this! And all of us today are included in this prayer, for His Majesty said, "Not only for them do I pray but also for those who will believe in Me through their word," and, "I am also in them."[88]

God, help me! How true are these words! And how clearly these words are understood by the soul that finds them fulfilled in this seventh Mansion. If it were not for our sins, we would all understand since the words of Jesus Christ, our King

---

[85] John 20:19-21
[86] Luke 7:50
[87] John 17:21
[88] John 17:20, 23

and Lord, cannot fail.[89] It is we who fail by not removing anything that stops this light. We must put an end to staring at ourselves in the mirror where our image is engraved.

Returning to what I was saying, God places the soul in His own Mansion, which is at the very center of the soul. They say that the highest heaven where our Lord dwells does not revolve with the rest of the universe. Similarly, in this Mansion the movements of our faculties and imagination can never injure the soul or destroy its peace.

Am I implying that the soul brought this far by God is certain to be saved and can't fall again? I do not mean this. Whenever I say the soul is secure, it is only for as long as His Majesty holds it in His care and the soul does not offend Him.

At least I know for certain that a soul does not consider itself safe even if it realizes it has been brought to the seventh Mansion and if it has been there for many years. The soul is more careful than ever to avoid committing the smallest sin against God. It is anxious to serve Him and feels constant pain and confusion at how little it does for Him compared to what it ought to do.

For the soul, these feelings are a heavy cross. The more difficult the penances it can perform, the better it feels. And true penance comes when God takes away health and strength while doing penance. I explained this before in the restlessness of the little butterfly. These desires come from the roots of the soul where it is planted. A tree planted by running water is fresh and fruitful. It is no wonder that these

---

[89] Luke 21:33

are the longings of a soul whose true spirit has become one with heavenly water.

Now, do not think that our faculties, senses, and passions are always at peace. The soul still visits other Mansions where there are times of struggle, suffering and fatigue. But as a rule, the soul remains at peace.

This center of the soul or spirit is hard to describe and even believe in. I think, sisters, that my inability to explain may save you from the temptation to not believe me. It is so hard to understand how we can have trials and suffering and yet experience peace in the soul.

Let me give you a comparison – may God help it to be useful. A king sits on the throne in his palace. Many wars and disasters befall his kingdom, but the king is still on the throne. In the same way, although storms, noise, and wild animals rage in the other Mansions, no one enters the center of the Mansion and makes the soul leave its peace. Nothing the soul hears will make it leave.

Although it wishes it did not have troubles, the suffering is not enough to disturb the soul or rob it of its peace. And passions no longer dare enter the soul – they know they would only be defeated if they tried.

In the same way, our entire body may ache, but if the head is sound, the head does not ache just because the body aches. I smile at these comparisons. They do not please me, but I can't find any others. Think what you will, I have spoken the truth.

Three

Transformation in the Seventh Mansion

The little butterfly has died with great joy. It has finally found rest and Christ lives within her. Let us see what has changed between her present and former lives. For from these effects, we will see if what has been said is true.

First, from what I understand, there is such complete self-forgetfulness that truly the soul seems to no longer recognize itself – it was rain that has now joined with a river. The soul does not dwell on the fact that heaven, life, and glory are theirs, because it is completely occupied with pursuing God's honor. The words spoken by His Majesty have done their work – if she cares for His affairs, then He will care for hers. There is no more worry about what may or may not happen.

The soul experiences strange forgetfulness, for it seems not to exist or want to become anything. But then it understands that something can come from itself which can advance the honor and glory of God, even if only a little. For this purpose, the soul would willingly die.

Do not think, daughters, that such a person forgets to eat and drink or attend to regular duties and obligations. We are only talking about what is happening inside these souls, where it suffers knowing how little it can accomplish through its own efforts. It wishes it had more strength to do everything in the world possible to honor our Lord.

The soul in the seventh Mansion has a strong desire to

suffer, but it does not disturb the soul as it did before. Now the desire for God's will to be done exceeds the desire for suffering. If He wills the soul to suffer, it is well and good. But if not, the soul no longer tortures itself with the desire for suffering.

The soul also feels great joy when it is persecuted. More than ever before, it experiences peace when this happens. It does not bear a grudge against those who do or desire to do it evil. The soul even has a special love for its persecutors and is saddened when they are in trouble. It does all it can to help them and earnestly asks God to intercede on their behalf. It would gladly give up favors from His Majesty if they could be given to others to prevent them from offending our Lord.

To me, the most surprising effect on the soul in the seventh Mansion is that it no longer feels sorrow because it cannot soon die and enjoy His presence. Sorrow is exchanged for a strong desire to serve Him. The soul only hopes that through its service others are helped or He is praised.

Not only has the soul stopped longing for death, but it wishes for a long life with many trials if this will bring the Lord greater praise. This desire is unchanged even with the certain knowledge that death will bring them immediate enjoyment of God.

Nor do they desire death so they can enjoy the glory of the saints. These souls understand that their glory comes from any help they give to Him who was crucified. They especially want this because they see how many people offend Him and how few are detached enough from the world to only care for His honor.

Of course, sometimes they forget this. They are overcome again with tender longings to enjoy God and leave this land of exile, particularly when they see how little they serve Him. But then the soul remembers that it already continually experiences His presence. With that it is content, and the soul offers its desire to live as sacrificially as it is able.

The soul fears death no more than it fears God's favor. The fact is, He who gave them these torturing desires for death has exchanged them for other desires. May He be forever blessed and praised!

The soul in the seventh Mansion also no longer desires consolations or spiritual delights. It now carries God within itself – it is He who lives. Clearly He led a life of continual suffering, and to be like Him souls in the seventh Mansion both experience and desire suffering. But in our suffering He leads us mercifully and as our weakness requires. And when He believes it is necessary, He gives us His strength.

Awakenings in the Seventh Mansion

These souls, being completely detached from everything, wish to either be alone or busy with whatever benefits the souls of others. They no longer experience spiritual dryness or interior trials. They live with a constant tender remembrance of our Lord and wish to never stop praising Him.

When the soul becomes distracted, it is awakened by the Lord in the way explained in the sixth Mansion. The soul understands that these awakenings from God come from the deepest part of the soul, and in this Mansion they are experienced gently. There is no reason to think the soul has anything to do with them because they are not produced by the mind or memory, and they become ordinary and frequent.

No matter how large the fire, flames always shoot upward. It is the same with the movement of these awakenings. They proceed from the center of the soul and ignite all the faculties. There may be nothing else accomplished by this prayer except knowing the special care God takes to communicate with us. Through these awakenings He gently asks us to abide with Him. All our past pain would be worth enduring for the sake of these sweet and penetrating touches of His love.

You have experienced this, sisters. I think once the Lord has brought us to the prayer of union, He watches over us with these awakenings unless we neglect to keep His commandments. When you receive these impulses, remember they come from this innermost seventh Mansion, where God dwells in our soul.

Praise Him sincerely when you receive them because it is He who sends you these messages. They are love letters, tenderly written in a code so only you can understand what He asks. Never neglect to answer His Majesty, even if you are occupied with something or engaged in conversation.

Our Lord may be pleased to send you this secret message in public, but it is easy for you to respond since your reply is entirely interior. Reply with an act of love or ask, as Saint Peter did, "Lord, what would you have me do?"[90] Jesus will show you how and when to please Him. Understand that He

---

[90] Acts 9:6

hears us and that His touch, which is so delicate, nearly always helps the soul be able to do what was asked with a resolute will.

Other Effects on the Soul

Another difference in the soul in this Mansion is that, unlike all the others, the soul hardly feels spiritual dryness or disturbances. The soul is almost always calm. It is not afraid that this interior peace is a counterfeit by the devil, but it has a settled certainty that this peace has divine origin. This certainty comes from what I said earlier – His Majesty reveals Himself directly to our spirit, not through our senses or faculties. He takes us to a place to be with Him where I doubt the devil dares enter and where our Lord would never permit him to enter.

The graces given to the soul in the seventh Mansion are not the result of its own effort. The only effort required by the soul is what it has already done in surrendering itself totally to God. Every way the Lord teaches and helps the soul in this Mansion takes place noiselessly and in quiet. It seems to me this resembles the building of Solomon's temple, where the work was done in silence.[91]

It is the same within this temple of God, this Mansion where He and the soul rejoice in each other in profound silence. The mind is not required to do anything since the Lord wishes it to be at rest here and only observe through a crack what is happening to the soul. Sometimes the faculties

---

[91] 1 Kings 6:7

are not allowed to see, but this is only for a short period of time. In my opinion it is not that the faculties are lost, but in their amazement they do not work.

I am also astonished that the soul in the seventh Mansion rarely experiences raptures, and when it does they almost never take place in public. They are not accompanied by a feeling of being transported or by a flight of the spirit. If a rapture is given, it is not caused, as in the past, by a special call to devotion, the sight of a religious picture or upon hearing a sermon or sacred music.

Before, the poor little butterfly was so anxious that anything caused it to take flight. Perhaps now the soul has finally found rest, or it has seen such wonders that nothing can frighten it now. Or maybe, since it is in such Company, the soul no longer feels alone.

In summary, sisters, I do not know the reason, but everything changes when God shows the soul this Mansion and brings it to dwell within. Whatever previously troubled the mind and was impossible to overcome disappears all at once. Maybe this is because the Lord has just strengthened, expanded, or developed the soul. Or perhaps for some reason only He knows, He wants to make public what He has been doing in secret within the soul. His judgments are beyond our understanding in this life.

These effects, along with all the other good fruits I have mentioned from prayers in other Mansions, are given by God when He brings the soul to Himself with the "kiss of the mouth" sought by the bride.[92] I believe in this Mansion her request is now granted.

Here overflowing waters are given to the wounded deer.[93] Here the soul delights in the tabernacle of God.[94] Here the dove sent out by Noah finds the olive branch as a sign of firm ground discovered amid the floods and storms of this world.[95] Oh, Jesus! So much of Holy Scripture teaches us about the soul's peace!

Dear God, since you know how important this peace is to us, grant that Christians will seek it! In Your mercy do not take this peace away from those to whom it has been given. For until You give them true peace and bring them to the place where we will have it forever, we live in fear. I say "true" peace not because this peace is not true, but that if these souls forsake God, they must begin all their struggles again.

What will these souls feel knowing they could lose so great a blessing? Their fear makes them more careful. They try to gather strength from their weakness so they will not abandon any opportunity to please God.

The greater the favors received from His Majesty, the more mistrustful these souls are of themselves. And since through His marvels they have come to a better understanding of their own misery and sin, they, like the tax collector, do not dare lift their eyes to heaven.[96]

---

[92] Song of Solomon 1:2
[93] Psalm 42:1
[94] Revelation 21:3
[95] Genesis 8:8-12
[96] Luke 18:13

Sometimes they hope they can die so their soul would be safe. But then, as I said before, their love immediately makes them wish to live to serve God. Every worry concerning themselves they give to His mercy. Other times they are crushed by thinking about all the favors they have received. They feel they could sink from the burden, like a ship with too heavy a load.

I promise you, sisters, these souls have trials, but trials do not trouble them or rob them of their peace. For the storms, like a wave, pass quickly. And fair weather returns because God's presence within them soon makes them forget everything else. May He be forever blessed and praised by all His creatures! Amen.

Four

Sisters, do not imagine that the effects of spiritual favors in the seventh Mansion are always with you. The Lord occasionally leaves souls to the weakness of their natures, and then it seems that all the poisonous creatures from the Castle moat and other Mansions unite to avenge the time the soul was not under their control.

True, these attacks only last a little while, maybe a day or so, and they are generally caused by some passing event. But during these disturbances, the soul learns again how much it needs the presence of God. For the Lord gives the soul the strength and resolution to never deviate from His service. Trials only seem to strengthen the soul in the seventh Mansion, and its heart never turns. Disturbances like this do not happen often, but our Lord wants the soul to remember its human condition. This helps the soul be humble and better understand how much it owes Him and should praise Him for the grace it receives.

Do not imagine that souls in the seventh Mansion are perfect because they have such strong determination and desire not to sin. Although the Lord helps them avoid intentional sin, they still have many faults and are saddened that they may be unaware of some of them.

They are also saddened by the sight of other souls going astray. Even though they have strong hope of being among those who are saved, they remember what the Holy Scriptures say about the fate of men like Solomon. Solomon was a favorite of God and spoke to His Majesty intimately before he turned away from God.[97] Remembering Solomon, they can't help but fear for themselves.

Let the person who feels most confident on this point fear the most, for "Blessed is the man who fears the Lord," as David said.[98] May His Majesty always protect us. Begging Him to never let us offend Him is the greatest security we have. May He be praised forever. Amen.

Why God gives Spiritual Favors

It is good to explain to you, sisters, the reason God gives so many spiritual favors to souls in this world. I am sure if you have been paying attention you understand that He gives spiritual favors to produce effects on the soul. I want to return to this to make sure none of you thinks He gives these favors just for our pleasure. This would be a great mistake.

I think His Majesty can give us no greater gift then to give us a life like His beloved Son – and we know that His Son suffered. Therefore, as I have told you often, I feel certain that spiritual favors are given to our souls to strengthen our weakness so that we are able to imitate Him in His great suffering.

We always find that those nearest to Christ our Lord suffer the most. Think of what His glorious Mother and apostles endured. And how do you think Saint Paul endured such great trials? From Saint Paul's example, we see that his strength

---

[97] 1 Kings 11
[98] Psalm 112:1

came from the effects of contemplation and genuine visions from our Lord. These visions were not his imagination or a lie from the devil. And did Saint Paul hide himself so he could enjoy spiritual favors and do nothing else? From what we know, he never took a day's rest. And he could not have slept much because he worked at night to earn a living.[99]

I am delighted by Saint Peter's response to our Lord when he met Him in a vision while fleeing from prison. Our Lord told Peter, "I go to Rome to be crucified again." I always feel a special joy when I read this. What effect did this vision have on Saint Peter? He went at once to Rome to meet his death. And it was no small mercy from our Lord that Saint Peter found someone to provide him with death.

Strength for Service

Oh, my sisters, the soul God chooses for His special Mansion should forget about their comfort, be unconcerned about personal honor, and be far from seeking the approval of men! For the mind fixed only on Him, as it ought to be, must forget itself. All its concern should rest only on how to please Him more, and when and how it can show its love for Him.

This is the end and aim of prayer, my daughters. This is the reason for the spiritual marriage whose children are always good works. Good works are the unmistakable sign that prove spiritual favors come from God.

What good is it if I make acts of devotion when I am alone,

---

[99] 1 Thessalonians 2:9

planning and promising to do wonders in the service of God, only to do the opposite when I have the chance to act? Of course, no matter what, spending time with God always does us great good.

Even when we are weak and fail to act on our plans and promises, sometimes God provides us the power to do so, despite how difficult it may be. When He finds these weak souls, He gives them a severe trial during which the soul does everything it can to resist the trial. But when the soul receives the benefits, it understands the Lord brings profit from suffering. The soul becomes less afraid and more willing to yield to Him in future trials.

When our actions fulfill our aspirations and promises in prayer, it does the soul the greatest good. And what cannot be acted upon all at once can be done little by little. These prayers are most beneficial when the soul must bend its will to fulfill them. Even within the corners of these little monasteries you will find many opportunities for these prayers.

This is more important than I know how to express. Fix your eyes on the Crucified One, and all will seem easy. If His Majesty proved His love for us with such great labor and suffering, how can you expect to please Him by words alone?

Do you know what it means to be truly spiritual? It means becoming a slave of God, branded with His mark, which is the cross. Since spiritual people give God their freedom, He can sell them as slaves to world, which is what He was. And this does not harm them, but it grants them a great favor.

Unless you make up your minds to become His slave,

never expect to make much spiritual progress. For as I have said, humility is the foundation of the entire Castle. Unless you are truly humble, our Lord, for your own sake, will not permit you to travel very high since you may fall crashing to the ground.

Therefore, sisters, take care to build a firm foundation by seeking to be the least and a slave of all. Look for ways you can please and help others, for it always benefits you more than them. Built on such strong rocks, the castle will not fall.

I repeat, your foundation must not consist only of prayer and contemplation. If you do not work to gain and practice virtue, you will never progress. Pray to God that nothing worse happens to you, because you know that to stop is to go back. If you love Him, you will never be content to come to a standstill.

Perhaps you think I am speaking about beginners, and as you progress spiritually it will require less work, so you can rest. But as I have told you, the only rest for souls in the seventh Mansion is the peace they feel within. They do not have outward rest, nor do they wish for it.

Why do you think the center of the soul sends out inspirations, or rather aspirations? To put us to sleep? No, no, no! The soul is waging a battle from within to keep the powers, senses, and body from being idle. When the soul did not understand the benefits of suffering, it was outside suffering with the body. Now that it understands the benefits, the soul has greater capacity to wage war from its center.

Perhaps suffering is the means by which God brings the soul to its center, and the Company the soul now enjoys gives it even greater strength. If, as David says, "With the pure You show Yourself pure," there is no doubt we are now one with the Almighty by a sovereign union of spirit with Spirit.[100] Strength will cling to this soul, and so we can now understand the strength of the saints to suffer and die.

It is certain that with the strength gained by the soul, the soul in turn strengthens all within the Castle, including the body that often seems to feel no strength. But the soul is fortified with wine "drunk in the cellar" where the Bridegroom brings the soul and will not allow it to leave.[101] Strength overflows into the weak body, just like nourishing food.

Indeed, the body suffers much while it is alive. Since our interior strength increases, the soul has more energy for work than the body is capable of. The soul pushes the body forward, for all it can do seems like nothing.

The strength for the severe self-denial of many of the saints must have come from this center, especially for Mary Magdalen, who spent her early life accustomed to luxury. It caused the zeal felt by our father Elijah for God's honor, and the desire of Saint Dominic and Saint Francis to draw souls to praise God.[102] I assure you, though they were forgetful of themselves, they must have passed through great trials.

This, my sisters, is what I want us all to pursue. To offer our requests and practice prayer, not for our own enjoyment, but so that we may gain strength to serve God. Let us not look

[100] Psalm 18:26
[101] Song of Solomon 2:4
[102] 1 Kings 19:10

for an easier path and get lost. It would be strange to think we can gain these favors from God by any road other than the one traveled by Jesus and all His saints. Let us not dream of such a thing.

Mary and Martha

Believe me, for the Lord to always be present in us, Mary and Martha must join together to show Him hospitality.[103] Mary can't sit at His feet and at the same time offer Him something to eat. Her sister Martha must help her. And the food we offer Him is that in every possible way we draw souls to Him so they may be saved and praise Him forever.

You will have two objections about what I just said. First, Jesus says that Mary chose the better part. But remember, before Mary sat at Jesus' feet enjoying His company, she had already done some of Martha's work by waiting on our Lord and washing and wiping His feet with her hair.[104]

And even though she did not care because she loved Him, do you understand how much Mary humbled herself? She was a woman of nobility, yet she traveled alone to follow Jesus and entered homes she had never been in before. Her behavior was criticized by the Pharisees and many others.

Since so many people bitterly hated Jesus, Mary's love for our Lord became a source of ridicule. People reminded her of her former life and accused her of trying to be a saint, since I am sure she gave up her rich clothing. Knowing how people

[103] Luke 10:38-42
[104] Luke 7:37-38

gossip about others with less status than her, there must have been many cruel things said.

I assure you, sisters, Mary received the better part after self-denial and many trials. Even the trial of seeing Jesus hated would have caused Mary terrible suffering. Think about what she endured witnessing the Lord's death and suffering His absence for the long years until her own death. You see, Mary was not always delightfully contemplating at the feet of the Lord.

Second, you may object to my saying that you have the ability or means to draw souls to God. You would like to do so, but you do not know how since you can't teach or preach like the apostles. I have often answered this objection, but maybe not while explaining the Castle of our souls. I will talk about it now because I know you want to serve Him and are often concerned about this.

I told you that the devil fills our thoughts with grand plans. We think that just wishing for impossible things is better than putting our hands to work serving our Lord. Your prayers are important, but you need not desire to help the entire world when you can help your companions. Helping your companions is better work because you are more obligated to them.

Do you think it is unimportant that you are humble and ready to serve your sisters? Your readiness to do this and your love of God is like a fire. It will light their love for God and cause them to try harder to be good. You could accomplish a great work by helping your companions, and it would be very pleasing to our Lord. By doing everything in your power, you would prove to His Majesty that you are ready to do more. And He would reward you as if you had gained many souls for Him.

If you say, "But my work does not convert souls because my sisters are already good," then I say, who has appointed you judge? The better they are the more pleasing their praise will be to God, and the more their prayers will help their neighbors.

Conclusion

Finally, sisters, I will conclude by saying we should not build castles in the air. Our Lord does not care about the importance of our work but the love with which our work is done. If we do all we can within our power, His Majesty will help us do more every day, provided we do not quickly grow tired.

Our life here is brief – perhaps shorter than you think. Give our Lord every sacrifice you can, interior and exterior. His Majesty will unite our sacrifices with those He offered His Father on the Cross. Our small sacrifices given in love will have great value.

My sisters and daughters, may it please His Majesty that we all reach the place where we can praise Him forever. And may He give me grace to practice what I teach you through the merits of His Son who lives and reigns forever. Amen. I assure you I am filled with confusion and beg you, for the sake of the same Lord, to remember this poor sinner in your prayers.

Epilogue

When I began writing this book I felt reluctant to begin, but now that it is finished, I admit the work has brought me much happiness. I think the labor was worth it, and I confess it did not cost me much.

My sisters, considering your strict confinement and the little recreation you have, I think it may console you to enjoy yourselves in this interior Castle. You can enter and walk about it at any hour you please, without asking permission from your superiors.

It is true you cannot enter all the Mansions by your own power unless the Lord of the Castle Himself brings you there. If you hit obstacles to entry, do not become angry or frustrated. This may displease Him so much that He never grants you entry.

He dearly loves humility. If you think yourselves unworthy to enter the third Mansion, He will soon grant you the favor of entering the fifth Mansion. If you serve Him well and often spend time there, He will draw you into the Mansion where He Himself dwells. And you never need to depart from this Mansion unless you are called away by the prioress, whose command God wishes for you to obey as His own. If, by her orders, you are often absent from this Mansion, you will always find the door open when you return.

When you have learned how to enjoy this Castle, you will always find rest, no matter how painful your trials may be. For you always have the hope of returning to the Castle, which no one can take from you.

Although I have mentioned only seven Mansions, each one contains many more rooms above, below, and around it.

Each contains fair gardens, fountains, labyrinths, and many more things so delightful that you will wish only to praise the great God who created the soul in His own image and likeness.[105] If you find anything in this which helps you know Him better, be certain it was sent by His Majesty to encourage you. Whatever you find amiss is my own.

In return for my desire to help you serve my God and Lord, I beg you, whenever you read this, praise His Majesty fervently in my name. Beg Him to prosper His Church, to give light to the Lutherans, to pardon my sins and free me from purgatory, where perhaps I will be by the mercy of God when you see this book. That is, as long as this book is given to you after it has been examined by theologians.

If these writings contain any error, it is because of my own ignorance. I submit in all things to the teaching of the holy Roman Catholic Church, of which I am a member and promise I will be in life and death. May our Lord God be forever praised and blessed! Amen, amen.

This writing was finished in the monastery of Saint Joseph of Ávila, in the year 1577, on the eve of the Vigil of Saint Andrew, for the glory of God who lives and reigns forever and ever, amen.

---

[105] Genesis 1:26

www.ingramcontent.com/pod-product-compliance
Lightning Source LLC
Chambersburg PA
CBHW071430070526
44578CB00001B/57